Mountain Secrets

Mountain Secrets

**Poems selected and edited by
Joan Fenney**

Mountain Secrets: Poems selected and edited by Joan Fenney
ISBN 978 1 76041 800 7
Copyright © poems individual authors 2019
Copyright © this collection Ginninderra Press 2019
Copyright © cover photo Ginninderra Press 2019

First published 2019 by
GINNINDERRA PRESS
PO Box 3461 Port Adelaide 5015
www.ginninderrapress.com.au

Contents

Introduction	Joan Fenney	11
The Mountain and the Eagle	Ian McFarlane	15
Fallen	Mary Pomfret	16
A question of peaks	Jude Aquilina	17
Biokovo, Tučepi, Dalmatia, 1943	Ann Simic	18
A Discovery	Suzanne Edgar	19
At the lookout	Jeanell Buckley	20
Binna Burra, not Byron	Jen Gibson	21
Grotto Point	Adèle Ogiér Jones	22
Lastours, France	Tracey-Anne Forbes	23
The Gully	Colleen Keating	24
No Killer Peak	Betty McKenzie-Tubb	25
Manus Island Detention Centre	Jill Gower	26
On the Road Near Molong	Cassandra J. O'Loughlin	27
Metamorphic rock	Anne M Carson	28
How to Move Meenhi	Julie Thorndyke	29
Unseen Memories	Airlie Jane Kirkham	30
Call of the Wild	Jocelyn Munro	31
Mandela on Its Mind	Virgil Goncalves	32
Gannets and Rainbows	Rose Helen Mitchell	33
Message in the Mist	Adriana K. Wood	34
dreaming time	Geoffrey Neville	35
The Keeper	Margo Poirier	36
The Source	Dorothy Hansen	37
The Lover's Eye	Lyn Reeves	41
coming down	jenni nixon	42
The View From Inside	Pippa Kay	43
Snapshots	Ray Liversidge	44
A Tourist in Te Aroha	Deb Stewart	45
Bushfires	Richard Bell	46

The Cloud and the Mountain	Colleen Moyne	47
Coming	Rebecca Law	48
You Are Mont Blanc	Michelle Gaddes	49
He Used to Climb	Millicent Jones	50
Beyond the ridge line	Christopher Hall	51
Canobolas	Mark Miller	55
iceberg	Jordie Albiston	56
Hearing the world, Wentworth Falls	Louise Wakeling	57
Icy Cinema	Irene Wilkie	58
Heat and snow	PS Cottier	59
Lost	John Egan	60
Everest	Jennifer Chrystie	61
Last Light	Jeff A. Harbrow	62
The Pipes and Drums	Margaret Zanardo	63
A Tune of Mt Oberon	Mark Cornell	64
The call of the Highlands	Rosemary Winderlich	65
The Snow Has Melted	Bernadette Anderson	66
Alice At MONA	Ann Nadge	69
The flag, of the word the	Joe Dolce	70
Walker	Gordon McPherson	71
Mal de pays*	Brenda Saunders	72
Woman	Natalie D-Napoleon	73
That Day on Tangkuban	Ros Schulz	74
Third Wish, kunanyi	Anne Morgan	75
Amber Puppy	Libby Sommer	76
At a Certain Age	Sue Cook	77
A sense of sovereignty…	Janey Mac	78
Meditating on G.M. Hopkins	Valerie Volk	79
Holding on	Gina Mercer	80
The Moan of the Currawong	David Atkinson	81
The Promised Land	Margaret Bradstock	82

Kingfisher	Kathryn Fry	83
In the foothills	Margaret Clark	84
The Hermit	Ian Coulls	85
Rock Solid	Donna Edwards	86
there's a shed load of pigs out there	Sandra Renew	87
Jagged	Decima Wraxall	88
Looking Back	Susan-Gaye Anderson	89
Swiss Alps	Shelda Rathmann	90
Questioning heaven	Martin Christmas	91
Mount Ainslie dreaming	Jennifer Sinclair	92
The Endless Summit	Jean Winter	93
Namadgi Peaks	Tony Steven Williams	97
Flinders Ranges	Jill Gloyne	98
Caspar David	Kevin Densley	99
Tai Shan	Mary Jones	100
Altitude	Roland Leach	101
a dream of Kunanyi	Thérèse Corfiatis	102
Brokenback	Adrian Lane	103
Guardians of the Altai	Adrian Rogers	104
Montacute in winter	Dawn Colsey	105
Time Belongim You, Massa	Danny Gardner	106
On visiting Stavrovouni Monastery…	Maureen Mitson	107
Gunung Batur	Indrani Perera	108
Once were sacred	Michael Thorley	109
all aflutter	Sarah Agnew	113
Legend of the Green Domes	Hazel Hall	114
Three References to Mountainsæ	John Watson	115
dunes, perlubie beach	Rob Walker	116
Valentine's Day 1900	Avril Bradley	117
Among Shadows	M. Fermanis-Winward	118
Silent Valleys	Barbara Fisher	119

The Citadel	Christopher Nailer	120
Haunting Cries	Brenda Eldridge	121
Day of Light Festival 299 BC	Anthony J. Langford	122
Mountainous Aspirations	Greg Tome	123
The Barrier	Colin Rogers	124
Red Hands Cave	Kay Hefferan	125
Fame	Geoff Graetz	126
birdwing	Anne Kellas	129
Descendings	Philip Radmall	130
Pink Champagne…	Melissa Bruce	131
Novice retreats: day 1	Steve Tolbert	132
this new moon	Tim Metcalf	133
You Yangs	Karen Throssell	134
After she left	J V Birch	135
Alone between sentences	Myra King	136
Cloud Dreaming	Lorna Thrift Brooks	137
The Wedge-tailed Eagle	William Cotter	138
Thinking Like a Mountain	John Weerden	139
alone unknown	Maureen Mendelowitz	140
Rosebery, West Coast, Tasmania	Graeme Hetherington	141
Our place	Mark Mahemoff	142
Coachwood Glen	Charles Freyberg	143
The view from below	Christopher Palmer	147
Because it's there	Marg Collett	148
Rock and Sky	Earl Livings	149
dolloped out there	Kevin Gillam	150
Tour de France	Fran Graham	151
Mount Field Shadows	Anne Collins	152
Waiting for Baby	Richard Stanton	153
Intrusion	Alice Shore	154
Gibraltar Ranges Ramble	Jacqui Merckenschlager	155

Crossing the Alps	Stephen Smithyman	156
Pauline Hanson's Bumslide Downward	Carolyn Cordon	157
Cresting the Peak	Max Merckenschlager	158
Endings	Jules Leigh Koch	159
Winter Shroud	ML Grace	163
Tar-Neem-Er-Ra	Dianne Kennedy	164
Sisters' Redress	Jane Carmody	165
Two-faced	Jeanette Woods	166
As I Air Punch	David Taylor	167
Tonight the Monaro storm comes…	Peter Hansen	168
Plain old rock cake	Louise Nicholas	169
In the High Country	Moya Pacey	170
A Great Ungreen	Maurits Zwankhuizen	171
Sublime Point	Brendan Doyle	172
Silk Road	Jean McArthur	173
Watagan Walk	Magdalena Ball	174
In Summer's Heat	Elaine Barker	175
My Milky Way	Maurice Whelan	176
Giant Stinging Trees	Jena Woodhouse	177
Aloof	Kristin Martin	178
Pursuing	Elizabeth Goodsir	179
Wellington Moods	Judith E.P. Johnson	180
Perspectives	Mark d'Arbon	181
Eagle on High	Barbara Gurney	182
Bush Trance	John Blackhawk	183
Flinders moon	David Harris	184
Wait Till You See Thirroul	Gabrielle Journey Jones	185
Reflections	Catharine Steinberg	186
Not everyone knows	Tass Holmes	187
to the pyramid	Jacqueline Buswell	188

Introduction

'Mountains know secrets we need to learn.' – Tyler Knott

Mountains are constant but continually changing. Captive to the seasons, they reveal many faces: in winter shrouded in snow and mist, yet so visibly majestic in the summer months that they appear to touch the sky. Lost in clouds at times, so discernible at others. Places of solitude yet at the mercy of mountaineers who swarm them. Both revered and feared; mystical and earthy; elusive but tangible. Does the mystery of mountains lie in the many paradoxes that surround them?

Mountains symbolise many aspects – overcoming obstacles, spiritual elevation, constancy, isolation and challenges. They inspire adventurers to scale their heights, and writers, lyricists, artists and photographers to portray them with words and images.

Secrets exist at the very core of mountains, while stories swirl around them. Poets are storytellers distilling these secrets and stories with an economy of words to capture the essence of mountains with memorable words.

With the mountains as a backdrop, Ginninderra Press poets have brought their creativity to this anthology, exploring themes of love, loss, hurt, courage, awe, reverence and solitude. Each poem in *Mountain Secrets* is original and reflects the poet's feelings about the subject. From 'mountains of ice', to a 'mountain as a staircase of stars', to the internal 'mountains of the mind', Ginninderra Press poets have taken us on a journey across the mountains with vivid and inventive images. The poems in the anthology are sometimes deeply personal, sometimes bold, sometimes humorous, but all invite the reader to consider mountains from a variety of perspectives.

Mountain Secrets is Ginninderra Press's seventh anthology since the press's inception in 1996. They are aimed at giving Ginninderra Press writers further opportunities to publish their work and to be part of a community of writers. The idea for the anthology was conceived by Brenda Eldridge, who was keen for GP writers to explore the many facets of mountains, in both a literal and figurative way. Once again, there was an overwhelming response from Ginninderra Press poets from around Australia to submit poems to the collection.

Thank you to Brenda for envisioning an anthology based around the thought-provoking subject of mountains and entrusting me to edit it. It has been a rewarding privilege to be part of the process. Thank you to all the poets who contributed so enthusiastically to *Mountain Secrets*. Thank you to Stephen for your ongoing support and Peter for being such a wonderful sounding board.

The launch of *Mountain Secrets* coincides with Brenda's seventieth birthday – a great occasion to celebrate two significant events. Happy birthday, Brenda, and may *Mountain Secrets* provide enjoyment and inspiration for all who read it!

Joan Fenney

'…Gulaga's ancient valleys
whisper secrets of their own…'

Ian McFarlane

The Mountain and the Eagle

In liquid light on wooded slopes,
Gulaga is weeping:
A Henry Moore sculpture
of a woman sleeping.
An eagle on the updraft
from Wallaga's sandy mouth,
mocks the law of gravity
with breezes from the south.
Waves curl towards the entrance
in question marks of foam;
the mountain and the eagle
are redefining home.
Flags of myth and moment,
and culture gathered wide,
shape a new republic's anxious hopes
from symbols of her pride.
But Gulaga's ancient valleys
whisper secrets of their own;
beyond the pale of history
and chilling to the bone.
The eagle falls with blurring speed;
dark blood rips the prey,
and dreaming in the sunlight,
bright shadows rim the bay.

Ian McFarlane

Previously published in *The Shapes of Light*, Ginninderra Press, 2014

Fallen

Faithfully I follow you up the trailing mountain track.
Trundling over rocks, you carry our fresh picnic lunch
Green salad, camembert and blush-pink wine.
Golden spring wattle taps your shoulders,
Anointing you with its sweet-scented blessings,
While I lug my barbed guilt, heavy and hurting.
Breathe it in, breathe it out.

Hurry up, you call, not knowing yet the secret I keep.
And you, gentle man,
Hold back a straggling branch for me to freely pass.
But you let it go too soon, accidentally of course, and
Runaway bough slaps my face which is, after all,
What I deserve for this closet I conceal.

You don't notice the red welt that streaks my cheek.

We are not mountaineers, you and I,
But our climb has been steep.
Without warning I stumble and trip on loose stones.
Oh, my angel, you have fallen, you say.

I am fallen, I say.

Mary Pomfret

A question of peaks

Is a mountain range's sharp bone blade
serrating sky, spearing cloud
over rain-trickle trees rattling shy ferns,
mosses, gully breath howling
glassy stream gnawing rock,
the meaning of mountain?

Does a solitary mountain, fog-haloed
dark guard of patchwork plains
sending messenger storms, shedding floods,
cool summer breezes, drawing eyes
yet hiding fox and platypus,
hold an ancient secret?

Are you a mountain, face weathered,
eyes fixed on some scene we cannot see;
river veins, heart granite-true –
landscapes you once knew now road-coated
to final peak, dawn climb, mist parting
to let you through?

Jude Aquilina

Biokovo, Tučepi, Dalmatia, 1943

The eyes of my mountain stare down to the sea
while I scale the perilous peaks circling their way
round the coast. Your gnarled hand soft on my
shoulder though you are no longer here. I climb
to the orchard you planted and tended, and drink
where we drank the burbling spring water.
They took you and shot you when I was just five.
Now I climb all alone your footfalls beside me.
Our home that you built high into the mountain
gazes down to the water and up to the peak.
Many caves mark my mountain, I squat in the
one by our orchard and by the cool spring.

I gather some grapes which I eat in the cave.
The mountain is sighing, I lean in his arms.
The mountain my father embraces his boy as
the juice of your grapes trickles over my chin.
I smell the smoke of your pipe as it drifts.
I watch you fashion a flute with your knife.
Your music seeps over our mountain, whispering,
murmuring, sobbing, as the sun sets over the water.
I scamper and slip down the slope to our home
where mother's dark eyes scour the mountain for me.
'Just walking,' I say, as I hand her some grapes
and hold secret my father my mountain.

Ann Simic

A Discovery

The mountain path is too severe
and more grey tors are looming above
so I stop my trudge from rock to rock
and veer away through wattle scrub
to huddled granite boulders.
From dark and gloomy burrows
the wombats trails go winding down
to a gully that's narrow and steep.

Here, all light in a twist of water sleekly falls,
ledge over ledge: secret, trickling, scintillant.

Suzanne Edgar

Previously published as 'Bush walk' in *Catching the Light*,
Ginninderra Press, 2019

At the lookout

Sweaty hands and a skip to the cool world outside the bus
Squelching fun in the mud of the car park
Down and down to the lookout, the blue and gold uniforms snake along the caramel p
A sweetness with no name wells in his mouth
Leaping over silver bright waters gurgling from above
It's the land of his storybooks where shy fairies peak from behind leaves
He is too young to be sad but the shapeless yearning of his baby life has returned.

Cars and teacher, school and parents, he gallops up the line from their grasp
His hand meets frizzled moss, wetness, damp pollen between his fingers
He has found the pocket of the world where his soul was born
This place is the mountain parent from the time before he became a human boy
The whispering damp, down and into wet thickness of overhanging breath and shivering fer

Teacher's hands on his shoulder want to pinch him back to the schoolroom he has l
A sunny clearing ahead and teacher's words like car noise
On again and he says sorry for this noise to this new friend from the life before
The track delivers him to the lookout and heaven's breath upon his cheeks
Teacher shoving a scarf at his neck is a strangling rope
He has found it now, the meaning of the crazy bunch of stuff called the world.

Beyond the fence, tiny wings down there where the land shouts secrets to his ear
A twisting glistening path in its depth where his new spirit friend calls him to play
Maybe this singing expanse is what the church man called god's house.
A climbing exhilaration as he escapes teacher's hands, leaping to the embrace of his true l

Jeanell Buck

Binna Burra, not Byron

I've no specific preference for 'the Sunshine State'
(no biased Banana Bender here) – excepting
it cradles the secret side of the Great Mountain.

Distantly reclining 'mid lush verdure, your
soft Heffalump-trunk pauses awhile in
ruminative contemplation to gaze Pacificwards.

At rest, Cook's Warning peak, is gentle Wollumbin, cloud-gatherer
two differing views:
> t'other side of the border he's aroused, masculine –
> a sharp-peaked phallus, pre-empting danger.

Give me a mountain crafted as reclining elephant
trunk-tilted in serene content and joyous gratitude.

Soul-Dreamer of this ancient land, you
remain yourself, both sides of this divided realm
   – pristine reflector of morn's first sun
announcing Australia's dawn over the millennia.

Jen Gibson

Grotto Point

You told me there was a special place,
a grotto on the way up to the summit
hewn into the rock on the side of the hill
long before any recollection.

You told me it was sacred up there
a place for your old people's spirits,
its secrets their belonging, and why
journeying
back to the place
gave them meaning,
ground for old stories
on visits as clan to the peak
listen, silent – bar for singing's echo
answering
ancient stones
formed before yesterday.

You told me singing and first birdsong
still holds the message of this place
on the mountain,
secrets new travellers can hear on the wind
if they wait patient
in the early unfolding of dawn.

Adèle Ogiér Jones

Lastours, France

Mist in the dawn swathes the Montagne Noire
Crows like black smuts of soot swim in and out
Wreaths of white air caress undulant firs
And the heavy haul of Cathar past
Is dreamily opaque

Then in the renting sun, the shroud is gone
Mauve morphs to avocado, lime and quince
Three towers of a once strong and mighty fort
Thrust through the haze, grim remnants of a proud
Culture cowed and slain

But from the fort, the view is now serene:
A clustered village nestled in the vale
Wild hillside sprouting iris, cistus, broom
And winding stone-flagged paths surveyed by tall
And patient pencil pines

With hazy fog or seeming tranquil ruins
The black mountain hides her dark secrets well.

Tracey-Anne Forbes

The Gully

      the creek chatters with small rocks
as it slithers along   decanted
from a swamp   succulent
as ten thousand soaking sponges
fringed with ferns   lichens   mosses
sedges   spotted with silver dew
      the rustle of a lyrebird
singing the land back to healing
mimics a birdsong world
and conceals a secret
a mountain secret
      there was a time in the Gully
when the lyrebird was silent
and the wind mimicked a deep howl
and the earth grieved and raged
for its evicted people
its ravaged concreted land
      today the lyrebird's song rolls back
a many-layered history
the Gundungurra and Darug people
lead us out of an amnesic fog
with a *remember* story –
      a redemptive pathway into now

Colleen Keating

The Gully: an Aboriginal place in Katoomba

No Killer Peak

no conga line to death

proud mountain, island icon
necklaced with rocks
fixed for aeons

only the mountain dwellers
know these secrets:
your peak in sunlight
while the grey city sulks below

swirls of vapour encircle houses
snow feathers soon will fall

the organ pipes –
no longer morning pink –
six-sided flakes
each marvellously different
veil their glow

there are grassy patches
where lovers can lie down –
remembering, make obeisance.

Betty McKenzie-Tubb

Manus Island Detention Centre

After *No Friend but the Mountains*, Behrouz Boochani (journalist and refugee)

there are secrets in the mountains
on Manus Island
secrets of the internment
of innocent asylum seekers

surrounded by jungle and tall wire fences
home is a small container
four men sharing each one
sweating non-stop in the tropical heat
suffocated by humidity
thirst unquenched with warm bottles of water
scarcely enough food or medical attention
cameras watching their every move
even in the toilet block there is no privacy

loneliness and despair are all they feel
dehumanised, their spirits broken
no hope, no beauty for the soul
many attempting suicide
too many succeeding

Behrouz Boochani had a mountain secret
finding some relief in the jungle over the fence
colourful flowers and birdsong
to dream about and lose himself in

Jill Gower

On the Road Near Molong

Wait for dusk when the boulders rooted in grassy dens
are silhouetted, the sky a faded cerulean blue in the cold
and fraying into the eucalypts of the Catombal Range.
See the ancient language written in the shaggy horizon
that swallows fences and roads. Listen
for the owl's long syllable, the zephyr's unshod steps.
Your body's profound obedience will respond
to the quiet dance already going on.

You can tell by the way the trees stand silent
in all that space the night owl descends into, homing,
that the secret of secrets is disclosed. You can hear
the far-off peaks saying things you can't endure
alone in the dark. Find yourself changed,
as if the wisdom misplaced at birth is in you again
questioning your entire warped nature. Trust the forces
that fire the world, the sentient world that contains us.

Cassandra J. O'Loughlin

Metamorphic rock

Gariwerd

The rock is adamantine Grampian grey, curved and coloured
like animal hide. We're fleas scaling the beast's flank,
hauling our body-sacks of dead weight. Climbing, clinging,

clambering – eyes always on the vertical, stubbornly insisting
against the downward pull of death. For now the rock
tolerates us, but just a twitch would fling us to the stony floor.

Lichens stain the rock in faded greens, pale pinks and blues –
a pastel patina. Tiny-filigreed petals unfurl into papery rosettes.
Like emerald mosses, tenacious in adversity, asking little.

Even in a hard place, fertility is various and kind. The heavy,
obdurate nature of stone is impossible to refute, its finality
of placement – here on the ground, hunkered down for millennia.

But movement is rumoured all around. Clefts and pleats
where rock was riven, then folded concertina fashion. Cliffs
plunge, rear. Sandstone boulders scooped and scoured by winds,

eons of weather. Rockfaces are shirred, smocked by seamstress
Time. Once rock was fluid, pliable – now solidified, eroding
slowly. Metamorphosis is the secret the rocks hold.

Anne M Carson

Previously published in an earlier form in *Pennsylvania Review*,
USA, March, 2013

How to Move Meenhi

Touch her, says the Wind. Bother her with sleek caresses,
massage every aching outcrop with persistent care.
Pull the tangled dry twigs from her hair and pummel the tired
sandstone boulders that shore up her resistance.

Wash her, says the Rain. Cleanse every private crevice
and deep limestone canyon with cool pelting drops until she is free
of drudgery and her ridges are covered with fresh green foliage,
flannel flowers bursting open like a thousand pale stars.

Warm her, says the Sun. Open every damp dark
moss-covered place to new light and heat. Dry her ancient
layers of shale and crack wide the steep basalt walls that have held
old knowledge in silence for far too long.

Woo her with words, says the Poet. Enfold her
in a garment sewn of kindness. Wrap a tender lacy shawl
of mist around her ironstone shoulders until she trembles
with desire and tells you every secret she possesses.

Julie Thorndyke

Meenhi: one of the Three Sisters in the Blue Mountains

Unseen Memories

Slipping from the edge of the city
I come upon the mountains,
tinged blue, misty, inviting.
I wander under a rainforest roof
like a tunnel in the mountain,
unseen by the eyes until it is chanced upon.
The path takes me along in silent steps,
in wonderment, as the light filters through the deep gully
revealing secrets well hidden.
Fungus peeks out of undisclosed holes.
I come upon a sparkling cascade.
Behind it, a secluded gem, a cave,
a place of shared secrets, of ancient origins from Gondwana.
Wonders, what history, what stories would it tell.
Droplets drip in a silver stream, staccato like.
That cascade then creeps down the gully over rolling stones,
denuded rocks, mossy crevices, craggy cliffs, sandstone boulders.
I find a secret place, a pool left deep from receding flood waters.
A bird finds its voice, a single voice choir,
a grey shrike thrush in melodious flute-like song.
Fairy wrens join in with answering trills a cappella.
The trees whisper, the grasses dance in the wind.
I linger, stand silently in this gully of long dreaming.
Spellbound, I confine these gems to my deepest dreams
before these moments slip away.

Airlie Jane Kirkham

Call of the Wild

The secrets of mountains stretch from their bases to the far away tops
they lie in crevices, rocks, and mosses
clinging tightly where seeds land and roots hold stubborn on windy slopes
whining their songs over grasses and scrub and tall forest trees
– stretching their limbs skyward
in adoration of the peaks above
the tall peaks – conclusion of ancient eruption.

The secrets of mountains are the calls to pull boots on
to toughen up and face the music
of wind in the trees soughing and sighing ancient secrets
as you haul yourself up, pack high on your back,
listening for the silence where the tree line ends
and the grasses sing the quiet draughts' shadows
when they rattle their seed heads –
a come again go again trace of whispers in hiding.

The secrets of mountains are the voices of the wild
which sit in the bones of those who listen
which curve and twist trails
in the minds of the seekers who hear them –
are the voices of the dreamers who conquer
the heights and their fears and feel free
to abandon the ties which could bind them
to the plains far below.

Jocelyn Munro

Mandela on Its Mind

From up high,
the mountain looks out

beyond menacing clouds that shroud it,
       towards the huddle of frayed blankets;

beyond violent rain that unleashes on it,
       towards the deluge of cheerless tears;

beyond exposed flora that tremble on it,
       towards the shiver of stripped victims;

beyond guiltless fauna that trample it,
       towards the crush of tortured souls;

beyond intrusive tourists who inspect it,
       towards the spite of evil interrogators.

From up high,
what secrets did Table Mountain veil as it looked out
beyond
clouds, rain, flora, fauna and tourists,
       towards
       the island prison that, for decades, trapped a man
       conspiring only to make the world a better place?

Virgil Goncalves

Gannets and Rainbows

At sunrise on an April morning, in a hotel room,
I pulled curtains aside.
For the first time, through sparkling windows,
I saw Mitre Peak.
My brain filled with questions
about the might and majesty of this giant rock.
What force gave a shape to you?
Did Poseidon shift tectonic plates and create
convulsions in Milford Sound?
Now, sturdy hiking boots
mix with feather-soft footsteps
to explore your scraggy exterior.
Hungry screeching gannets make sanctuaries
in the crevices and craters on your surface.
Cirrus clouds floating above you
echo the shape and shade
of ice-white foam swirling at your base,
hiding the secrets of your beginning.
Ribbons of falling water roll from your peak,
then join forces with a friendly sun
to dress you in rainbows
of indigo, red, green and azure blue.
Among lesser craggy hills,
YOU claim lordship.

Rose Helen Mitchell

Message in the Mist

Across the ages my spirit seeks out my highland ancestors.
They trudge from coastal village to village seeking work,
Donald weakened by TB, wife Mary by his side.
Eventually, with their children, they will board a ship,
> *The Douglas*, headed for New Zealand,
>> Part of the mighty Scottish diaspora.

In New Zealand hardy pioneer Alex Sutherland has prepared a way,
Providing refuge and home for widowed Mary,
Granting a future to her children,
> My ancestors.

In the same spirit my grandfather provided a home for my war veteran father
> my mother and family and ME.

Today prosperous descendants forget the legacy,
Wrought from our ancestor's stoical Highland spirit that never gave up,
When Highland farmers were
> driven
>
> from
>
> their crofts.

Huge farms were created for profit at cost of the Highlanders' way of life.
The eternal mountains majestically rise to the clouds,
> Casting deep, long shadows
>> that reach to the present d

Hiding ancestral secrets.

Adriana K. W.

dreaming time

Yesterday dreaming my mother's blood
we saw those strangers come
like stars up above
They came from Sydney town newly rose
from convict ship and whip and toil
they fouled the soil
The cry of where do we go rose loud
louder than the voice of the whip
He took the chance
born free yet the poor were governed
Spread your wings, run lad run

Mountains rose like a shield
a barrier to heaven's gate
Sacred sites and ancient rites
We showed them the secret
of the Dreamtime trails we used
and plants abundant
Who believes the magic?
The might of nature's choice
the whisper of wind
the voice of the streams
Trudge like a snail
or march like a new day
But my sacred sites remain

Geoffrey Neville

The Keeper

I open my heart to you who rest
at my feet, to you to climb my slopes,
to you who perish in my crevasses.
I keep your secrets as I keep my own,
suffering wounds from too many steps
gouging paths that spoil my majesty.
I weep while being the perfect hostess,
anxious lest my strength may one day fail.
My most painful secret lies within my soul,
as I struggle with the many demands made of me,
my tears falling as snow from my crowning glory,
my music beating strongly within the rumble
of my core,
my head now spinning
with the sadness of humanity yet
I cannot betray any of these secrets
lest I falter and
lose
my power
forever.

Margo Poirier

The Source

For generations they had gone to the holy mountain.
There in the past they had sensed that there they would find
Answers, secrets that were never revealed in the hot,
Dusty plains. From here the elders had told

Them they would return and never be the same.
At full moon when the light shone on the peak
And the stars blinked their truth, it seemed
That the Spirit who created them would surely

Speak to them. The markings were all around them.
When the lightning struck, the thunder boomed, they thought
There had to be a secret place somewhere,
A place of certainty. They had seen signs but no one gave

More than hints about the secret at the top
Of the mountain from which the ancestors had returned
With shining faces. Who had they met there?
There had to be a mystery that explained the sea,

The rivers, the beauty that exploded each spring.
So the wise still tread upward, pressing for answers
Even to pain, fear and human loss,
Light after darkness, hope after the climb.

Dorothy Hansen

'I knew a man who wrote
his lover into the mountain…'

Lyn Reeves

The Lover's Eye

I knew a man who wrote
his lover into the mountain
when she could no longer climb
its tracks, hot with the scent
of eucalypt and pepperberries.
But words could not push back
the shadow, like the fist of a giant
ramming his chest, or stop
the clouds catching in his throat,
the ice entering his veins.

When you look through the lens
of a microscope or with the focused
eye of a lover you can read
the mountain's dreaming.
Through separations and migrations,
long winters, seasons of refuge,
traces remain: inscribed in leaves,
the breath of small white petals,
the folded hills, and boulders freckled
as a shoulder bared to the sun.

The black currawong, patient
on a fire-whitened branch,
bears it in his wings.

Lyn Reeves

Previously published in *Island* #91

coming down

icy winds bring down branches laden with snow
white magic thickly spread on the ground
the cold bites his skin   his breath floats in air
he smacks his gloves together
thoughts stilled as a frozen lake
early morning Qigong   smooth and calming
the kitchen tidied   everything in its place
leaving Katoomba in the Quiet Carriage
watching a young man eat crunchy cereal
scrape the plastic container   lid *clicks* with a resounding *snap*
a layer of milk settles on lips like a sprinkling of snowflakes
and he's remembering empty white sheets   his lover   the absence
a man reads the *Sydney Morning Herald* rustling the newspaper
he unfolds and carefully refolds the pages
a woman blows her nose into tissues
soon three people are sniffling   snuffling   sneezing
slowly the train rocks along the tracks   he almost yells
enough already this is supposed to be the Quiet Carriage!
the sun risen by the time he reaches his destination
he appears shrunken in his woollen overcoat
he's sweaty with too many layers of warm itchy clothing
exhausted   he pushes his way through busy turnstiles
into the clamour of yet another day in the city office

jenni nixon

Also published in *Rochford Street Review*, October 2019

The View From Inside

A false promise of mighty mountain views.
But from my window only swirling fog
and silence. I can hear my own heartbeat
and breath. The glass is cold and I'm confused
by warmth; the fireplace; a burning log.
The safety of electric light and heat.

Last night over cocktails I'd hoped you'd
tell me one more time how much you loved me.
But you confessed, said you loved another.
You left me in this murk for someone who'd
captured your heart and taught you how to ski.
Now I'm cocooned in a quiet bother.

Frozen inside despite the warmth. Crazy
enough to kill you, but stupid enough
to love you. Still. Pretend there'll be more,
that it's only a fling, like the way she
zigs and zags down the slope. Your bit of fluff.
Your new love will run off in the spring thaw.

Pippa Kay

Snapshots

Not sorrow breaks the heart / But an imagined joy, 'On a
Deserted Shore', Kathleen Raine

On those mornings you always seemed to wake before
The alarm, as if your biological clock was set to some
Troubled time that startled you from sleep
And started you on a chronological journey of grief.

Around every corner, along every road, down every highway
Every house you passed seemed blessed with domestic bliss,
Every room in every house holy with conjugal joy, every line
Of every love-gone-wrong radio song written just for you.

'Are we there yet?' You remember her tired attempts
To explain that desire can destroy any notion of distance
While imagining Lawson asking Wentworth the same question
And a gobsmacked Blaxland before mountains of blue.

And she – one of three sisters – turned to stone
Amongst blue and scribbly gums of the spur,
The Great Dividing Range a blur on the landscape,
The children like birds foraging in leaf litter at her feet.

Sometimes I caught her in those holiday moments, but couldn't
Hold her – and now regret I took the offer of a second set
Of prints and not another roll of film. Those photos
Are somewhere in this house, and – to this day – remain unframed.

Ray Liversidge

Previously published in *The Divorce Papers*, Mark Time Books,
2010

A Tourist in Te Aroha

New Zealand, 1999

I stand, with my camera poised, in the busy street
gazing up at Mount Te Aroha, *mountain of love*,
at the way it wears this morning's sun –
a crown of rays, ferried down
shadowed slopes in haze of light.

I can't capture on film the hazy beam
that stirs warm trickles of joy
through solar plexus, swirls to fingertips,
floods me with a sense of home
as though my blood had known its myth.

I am only a tourist passing through.
The road is a thief
stealing me for its false pilgrimage
when everything whispers 'stay',
and I long to reach the summit of such love.

Deb Stewart

Previously published in *The White Line of Language*, Ginninderra Press, 2019, *Slow Notes*, Ginninderra Press, 2008, and in *Shadow Selves*, Ginninderra Press, 2003

Bushfires

The Glenbrook fires have long gone.
They laid siege to our lives in sixty-eight
but were held – they retreated
leaving us an empty world –
and future memories.

Still warm grey ash underfoot
and black scars on my sleeves
where I brushed against a charred tree;
on this fire-emptied hillside,
no birds sing.

Your death was also such a fire
that swept through my mind so many years later.
Some fires cannot be extinguished.
This was one, I had to wait years
for the ashes of my anguish to cool,
and hope the phoenix of our life together
would rise again, in poems perhaps.

As then, slowly waddling across my path
in the post-fire devastation on that hillside,
a small and dusty, unthinking echidna
came from nowhere,
out of the cooling ashes.

Richard Bell

The Cloud and the Mountain

We sit together beside the lake
immersed in quiet conversation,
you sharing the wisdom of your years,
me harvesting each precious word like ripe fruit.

In the distance an ancient mountain
stands like a ziggurat against the blue sky.
We watch as a downy cloud sidles up
and wraps itself lovingly around the peak.

I smile at the thought
that you and I are much the same as they.
You are the mountain, steadfast and unshakeable
and I am the cloud, soft and yielding, ever-changing.

And yet, together, the soft and the strong
form a bond that is meant to be,
and just like the cloud and the mountain,
together we are a force of nature.

Colleen Moyne

Coming

A man tries to say farewell
by walking in winter shoes
and clothes the downhill
of a beach embankment,
negotiating the moist, heavy
sand a fair portion of the
shoreline. His thirtyish
hands half in each of his
trousers side pockets, a gaze
that wants to look forward
but confessionally looks down
regularly; and this way speaks.

A journeyer climbs down
a mountain, the summit's
revelatory light and true, utmost perfection
held as if there were only one heart
one could love for a lifetime

And there appears to be
singing from females with high voices
as in a chant from another land

and home feels as vast as the whole of earth
but invariable in offering peace.

Rebecca Law

You Are Mont Blanc

for Mehmet

10 a.m.: '*Écoute, Je t'aime. Je t'aime.*'
Your landscape is fresh, scarred and eloquent; high
with seasons I do not know –
Your face finds its way through the morning
light of my winter morning, I am
Blinded, stupefied by your love
sent from the deepest northern midnight.
Your tunnelled summit is firm and pure.
Our sharpened shadows explode inside my follicles so
I stow the ordinance inside my hidden, powdery canyon.
You are Mont Blanc – your
Strength, your Mighty Force
shakes the foundations of my unearthly soul.
Your wildest avalanche has rocked
me rotten. I face the west –
your boiling snow courses through me,
melted beyond the primal stratum.
For, when your deluge floods, ravages,
I drink it –
to the welcome death.

Michelle Gaddes

He Used to Climb

he used to climb mountains
once – his sad sigh
whispered to me –
how easily he took each stride
bounded with the energy
of bursting champagne
just yesterday it seems
but today when he walks
the gentle rise yesterday becomes
a hazy maze of mean dreams

now all the energy he owns
is barely enough
to climb the sullen red path
step after leaden step until,
forced to stop, he can
remember proudly
and know with the strength
of the depth of a deep pool,
that he is still that man
who used to climb mountains

Millicent Jones

Previously published in an earlier form under the title 'Yesterday' in *The Bird of Time*, Kendall, NSW, 2018

Beyond the ridge line

Cradle Mountain

Snake trees inscribed
with lichen tales, trails that lead
to rosewood polished pools
The tangle-foot fagus

falls from green and gold to red
here, we find all the seasons
and rivers fed from way above
Currawong scrapes his metallic song
along the rusted belt of sky

and through moss and scrub,
light on foot we follow fly
Bleached white trunks abound,
rare trod ancient ground, eyes
stare out the blinking earth
And finally, we tread where river flows

quiet with all its thought wrung out
Look beyond the ridge line,
look: beyond the scree,
where great King Billy pines his love
and all the world can see.

Christopher Hall

'…the Mountain's song of ice…'

Mark Miller

Canobolas

We follow the track from the summit to the Falls,
our heads now out of the clouds,
our bodies anaesthetised by the cold.
In the drizzling rain we slip,
dislodging stones,
sending them clattering before us
as the cliff walls stare implacably back.

At the Falls,
we clamber over black volcanic boulders,
our tumbling words
seeming to lose themselves
in the stream's soft-rippling coil
and rocks below.

Soon, a slick wind scythes upwards
from the ravine's undergrowth of shrub
and we search for the track in mist,
feeling tired and vulnerable,
listening and almost hearing on the wind
the Mountain's song of ice,
its ancient volcanic murmurings
beneath our breathless footfalls back
to the summit and the car.

Mark Miller

Previously published in *This Winter Beach*, Seaview Press, 1999

iceberg

how lovely she looks   A-68   in
her frills & flounces & floes   as she splits
from family & Larsen Ice Shelf &
splinters & off she goes   it is a white
wedding as convention calls   & Father

Time arrives on time to give his daughter
away   Wiki proclaims there is 'no pre-
dicted path at this point'   no sense of fate
at this stage   no matter   the bride is dressed
in tatted perfection   her lacework face

astounds   & despite observations that
forecast destruction on all domestic
& universal grounds   she sees the good
sea & the good sea is warm   & with a
galumph she marries & melts in his arms

Jordie Albiston

Hearing the world, Wentworth Falls

Mid-mountain, you feel the weather coming in, drifts of fog
and nimbostratus infiltrating from the Southern Highlands.
Past the village sign you know you're home, behind you
the four-car prang, blue flashing lights, the glitter and crunch
of debris on the road. Tonight, you're unscathed. Clouds
are gravid with tomorrow's snow. All the forecasts agree,
an extreme weather event is on the cards, though the Bureau
calls it 'cold front' not 'Antarctic vortex'. Pity – you like
the drama and magnitude of it, global weirding
with a vengeance. It still takes you by surprise next morning,
hyperreal, the world transformed, and you, in that moment.
Padding across the yard, Frieda leaves dark lacunae, spoor
disappearing into white-out. You wonder if the Falls below
are poised in ice, a Hokusai wave about to shatter.
Suddenly, driving becomes a dangerous idea, like strapping
explosives to your chest on a crowded street. Why risk it
for your workaday routine, coming down from the mountain
to the flat plains of what you do for a living? You make
the necessary call, rake in the windfall of a day at home.
Maocat peers under Roman blinds at ghost-white trees,
a stretch of unfamiliar lawn. The flight of birds is stilled,
their startled childlike cry, Buddha fountain silent
among the ivy. Half-closed eyes look inward and outward,
long earlobes hear what's needed in the world

Louise Wakeling

Previously published in an earlier form online as one of three
highly commended poems in the 2018 Bruce Dawe National
Poetry Prize

Icy Cinema

To stand among mountains
at the head of a valley,
to look out into space where
ice-clouds crystal on the wind
glistening the first approach
of winter's cinematography,
to face new snow sweeping
the high air so fast we clench our fists
ready to meet it on a stark cliff edge,
to see the yellow sun light this tongue of wrath
seething toward us, dank underbelly growling
through the arms of ironbark,
to see the hawk bank and turn before the gale,
the waterfall curl its mist in long streamers
of errant draught
is to shout that we are the only ones
in this place, on this spur
to greet the snow's first drum roll,
the only ones embracing
the gold, the white
the purple, the black
about to wrap us in breath so sharp
the freeze will be as flame.

Irene Wilkie

Previously published in an earlier form in *Extravagance*, Ginninderra Press, 2013, as a part of a longer poem, 'The Mountain Has Many Faces'

Heat and snow

Mountain pygmy possum

Such delicacy among hulking man-sized boulders,
this mere comma of curved tail, skiing out behind
a swollen plum of grey and brown. Fluorescent shouts,
muffled by iced white, reach dozing batwing ears below.
You wait out the winter, under parallel metal tracks
of sport, beneath a thousand pumping growling parties
and hungover oceans of thrown-back flavoured schnapps.
To a bogong, this powder puff is a nightmare predator
of sharp teeth and vampire appetites, who scuttles
back to burrow before sun warms tourists' dreams.
Sun may yet melt more, steal the cold pale blanket
that wraps you in long stretching rest, and gently
pillows you in that larder of deep-set sleepy stone.
For now though, and hopefully forever, your slowed,
sluggish heart punctuates soil like snowflakes,
tapping on frozen slopes above. Mini metronome
still counts out the ages, measuring the months until
moths and seeds spring again, to pink grasping hands.

PS Cottier

Previously published as 'Mount Pygmy-possum' in *Cooma Feast of Poetry*, 2008, and in *The Cancellation of Clouds*, Ginninderra Press, 2011

Lost

The cold's ferocious in these mountains
and has been well before anyone came here.

The peaks are locked in year-long snow
and the dark forests engulfed in mist.

Grass never appears before the solstice
and the leaves fall in early August.

It is easy to lose oneself searching
among the forests where there is no sky.

John Egan

After Han Shan (Cold Mountain) between the 7th and 9th centuries

Previously published in *Mist and the Rose*, Ginninderra Press Pocket Poets, 2019

Everest

Black fingers clutch the icy crag
His gloves are shredded, his clothes wet through
He's coming home in a body bag

Down in the valley he made the brag
he'd be the first to see the peak view
Black fingers clutch the icy crag

Halfway up, breathless, he started to lag
his legs ton weights, his face grey-blue
He's coming home in a body bag

When he passed a corpse holding a flag
he realised the damage ego can do
Black fingers clutch the icy crag

They turned up the oxygen, carried his swag
but his speech was slurred. It was then they knew
he'd be coming home in a body bag

The highest mountain, the hardest drag
only existed for him to subdue
Black fingers clutch the icy crag
He's coming home in a body bag

Jennifer Chrystie

Previously published in *Weight of Snow*, Ginninderra Press, 2013, and in *Earthworks*, ed. Jean Sietzema-Dickson, a Poetica Christi anthology, 2007

Last Light

Last light silhouettes
eucalypt limbs
against a Highlands sky.
The fire churns out smoke
in a hard-fought battle
against the winter night.

The joints of my fingers groan in protest
and my breath hangs in the air
conversing with the steam from my enamel cup.

Jeff A. Harbrow

The Pipes and Drums

Through the mists I hear you calling
through the skirling of the pipes
with their tartans of Macdonald of the Isles –
ringing through the craggy summits
of the towering mountain peaks,
they echo round the lochs and mountainsides.

And I hear you marching closer
through the rattling of the drums,
your footsteps treading firm on ancient stones,
and the notes drift far above you
to the grey-stained autumn clouds
and longingly the music sings and hums.

Now the kilts sway step by step to reach
the castle gate on high –
there's a twirling of the baton and a stay –
and the pipes play long and lonely
on a shrill and quivering note
as you join the highland gathering in the sky.

Margaret Zanardo

Previously published in *Positive Words*, April, 2018

A Tune of Mt Oberon

Dusty grey-blue Mt Oberon
slumbers below the long
stretched sheets of an overcast sky.
Dark arms of a storm brew
rains upon the horizon as you
watch the fishermen slowly ply
the quickening waves to reach
their nets flung upon the fading white beach.
A webbed moon dangles through the gloom
a black rock bursts like a whale's backbone.
You've dropped next to me whispering a tune
which glides above the twilight shore's silver foam.
A song; hundreds of miles away from home,
rises behind my blue eyes, hauls my lazy bones
up to capture this rhyme before it's flown.

Mark Cornell

The call of the high country

I have felt the mountain's breath
the mountain's tears
the mountain's song is in my ears
wind, bird cries and rushing streams
and now it seems
I must return to the flat and wide
and home calls as I westward ride
heart full of mountain dreams.

This flat land has beauty too
features more subtle, browner hue
and if I lived in that mountainous place
I might long for this brown land
far views, distant horizons, space
perhaps…but now
my heart resounds with a different song…
how could I stay away so long?

Soon, very soon
I will turn back to the highlands again
to refresh my spirit
inspire my pen.

Rosemary Winderlich

Previously published as 'Mountain Song' in *Larks, Lanes and Memories*, Ginninderra Press, 2019

The Snow Has Melted

The mountain trembles
as timid and nimble-footed horses
weave their way
through crooked snow gums
toward the valley below.

First mares and foals,
then the stallion
descend like a stream trickling.
As the ground levels
they stretch their bodies into a canter
under the gaze of the fresh spring sun,
before coming to a halt
by an icy stream.

The stallion stands afar
keeps watch on his herd in the rich green valley
while beyond his world
small men in small spaces
hold their pens
above dotted lines
to sign the cull of wild horses.
The mountain trembles.

Bernadette Anderson

'…The depths and mountains of the mind.'

Ann Nadge

Alice At MONA

Museum of Old and New Art, Hobart

Alice steps through the wonderland
Sandstone depths in MONA's
Underground mountain of Art
Past the Chamber of Pausiris
Cow carcasses, sarcophagi

And bright mounted butterflies.
In the glass and steel labyrinth
Her heart is cantilevered through
This strata-lined rabbit hole,
Time distorted by the false light

Of digital cherry blossom
And whispered waterfalls of sound.
Alice finds no mad hatters here
Only creative souls who climb
The depths and mountains of the mind.

Ann Nadge

The flag, of the word the

*t*he
flag, of
the word
the, flutters
on the summit
of the Thought-
Mountain which
is appearing through
the white clouds of this
blank page as we descend
in circles on the Word-Path
which   narrows in   sections
and if we   are careful   to
step   over   gaps   and
c r um b ling...   p or t ions...   of
t ra ck... moving slowly down ward
one step at a time, one word at a time,
not losing concentration lest we put
a foot wrong or drift off into unpoetic
rambling (like the last couple of lines) or
stumble into incoherence like *rhadaf
kendio filiflatus errrrrr...* like that, but walk-
ing care fully and mind fully, we soon
reach the bottom and looking back at the flag,
of the word the, fluttering waaaaaaay up on the
peak we see now how *ah! the Thought-Mountain
has   transformed   into   a   Word-Mountain!*

Joe Dolce

Walker

A scaffold for the newly aged,
it frames her white grip
as she lifts each leg
against the lust of gravity,
her cautious wheels turning
through the heartless fractures
of her years,
the relentless gradient
of the nursing home
halting her breath.

But she pushes on again
through the thin air
of her condition
and when at last we sit
under the dazzling lights
of her impossible zenith,
she recalls her youthful steps
and here on the roof
of her new world,
they dance as keepsakes
on the head of a pin.

Gordon McPherson

Mal de pays

On a mountain packed with snow
we search for the cascade gelée,
a spectacle of water and air frozen
in time. Each droplet shapes a tear
caught in the moment of falling.
Ice crystals freeze, hang as tapers
along a cliff-face, a mist rises,
particles hover in space.

Silence chills the sounds of winter.
An ice pillar creaks, falls
with the weight of heavy water.
Even the spill has iced over,
fallen debris sealed under glass.

It is Christmas in Switzerland
and the world has turned white.
Somewhere outside this blankness
I hear the chatter of foreign words
I'm lost in the muffled stillness
of a quiet despair. A white-out deeper
than winter slips like a snowdrift
drowning in me.

Brenda Saunders

Mal de pays: homesickness

Woman

A response to the photo book *Woman: A Celebration*, by Peter Fetterman

We weep for you when you die in your wars,
hang our heads, bury them in our arms, we wear veils, we bury ourselves alive,
get fat and old and happy, and drink and laugh, heads thrown back lusty and full,
tend to roses in a vase by a window, chenille curtains, light and shadows filtering through,
stare at waves alone on the shore, hand-woven reed basket in hand,
flee a dust storm, both hands grasping white school hats like eggs on pre-pubescent heads,
dance in circles, our skirts marking grooves in the air as we spin like record players with sure needles),
bake bread, fry frites, grin at the beauty of a song,
lose our skirts on the roller coaster at the funfair,
in Rome burns, we grasp each other and stare out windows at the flickering lights,
wash ourselves in a basin at Provence, worn shuttered windows, naked, unafraid,
nurse our children hidden from view,
kiss men goodbye at train stations, wave, stand alone and wait,
look into mirrors and braid each other's hair,
walk through mountains boom box in hand, long flowing skirt swiping the heads of dead flowers as we trek by,
gaze out windows in silhouette, our heads turned away, cut off from view,
sit under sun-bleached steer skulls grasping dead tree logs,
bend our knees and confess to priests as if we are lovers,
hold up the clouds and the sky with our hands,
pick apples in orchards,
crack pomegranates open,
the mountain
wait.

Natalie D-Napoleon

That Day on Tangkuban

That day I spent with you on the volcano,
mother and daughter, two solitary tourists,
I'd planned the way the words would spill –
the path we'd take wound gently in my mind,
meander along the rim of the crater
volcano still active, puffing fumes
like a satisfied smoker – in sight of the action
testing, testing, keep the pace to a stroll.
Roots from aborted trees blown out of soil
stood up like acrobats doing handstands.

Squatting on the grey ash clearing
we looked across the smouldering crater,
to the track edged by a rickety rail,
to the rows of warungs and the patient faces
poised with their smiling 'datang'
knowing we'd be coming back.
Did it take all this to say
the things we didn't say at home?
I heeded the fumes, skirted the smoke
left it for another day.

Ros Schulz

Tangkuban Parahu: crater in West Java
warung: eating stall
datang: welcome
Previously published in *Poetrix*, 2008

Third Wish, kunanyi

for KL

Remember the light on the Silver Falls track?
How it shimmied the leaves of the blanket bush,
ushering us to the reigning swamp gum
with its high-twigged raptors' nest?

You, the light-boned poetry sprite,
curved your walk to a dance
when we reached the caged-in wishing well.

I listened for stone tape voices
reverberating in the throat of the well –
stonemasons freed from the chafe of leg irons,
or muwinina laughter, cruelled to silence.

We circled twice for selfish wishes,
success in love and art.
My third wish gleamed like an 1868 threepence
minted in the snowmelt and rain that freed
Hobart Town from its scourge of foetid water.
I wished for mountain days unshackled.
Then. Now. Forever.

Anne Morgan

Amber Puppy

What can an amber puppy mean in a world of Siris and driverless cars?

I was older, one of the Baby Boomers. Life was a series of warnings: *Don't fall over rugs or loose cords, don't overeat, don't go to bed before nine, drink coffee after midday, watch too much Netflix.* When the new puppy arrived one birthday, rich brown as a rais[in], I heard it shadowing me: *Don't trip on the dog's lead.*

There was much to be anxious about. One day, walking along the mountain pa[th] the rain had eased, spring waterfalls spilled into the creek, soon we would cool off un[der] the trees – I lost my grip on the lead. Into the bushes he fled, disappearing into green[.] Since when did mountains swallow small dogs? I drove home in a frantic car. My be[st] friend. I'd loved him and he'd loved me.

The days staggered past like drunks. I prayed silently, absorbed sunshine, clim[bed] steps, wrote Letters to the Editor. *Don't panic, don't shallow breathe, don't think th[e] worst* – you could hear it all around. A reclining Buddha could show you how to deep[en] the breath. A bird call at first light could tell you when to get up. A storm could remem[ber] to fill the dams and the water tanks – I was meandering between the trees when I saw h[im] scampering through the creek. Splashing around then shaking himself dry. A muddy escapee. A barking survivor.

Where had he been these three long days? I could wash him, wrap him in a tow[el,] take him home. Unexpected good news could still happen. Dogs off-the-leash need[to] stay close to their mistresses. Trees shed their leaves in winter and dogs run away, b[ut] find their way back. Seventy-two hours later, what can an amber puppy tell you in [a] world of Botox and identity theft?

See the difference between holding on and losing your grip.

Libby Somm[er]

Previously published in an earlier form in *Quadrant*, September, 2019

At a Certain Age

She has peaked in her most mature years –
after her ascent of life's steep gradient
this privileged position at its apex
leads her to a mountain-top revelation –
it is not the vision of the promised land of Moses
nor the divine vision of racial harmony of Martin Luther King
nor even the 'vision splendid' of A.B. Paterson's Clancy –
rather her epiphany, a realisation, a relief:
no need from now to struggle ever upwards,
nor search for constant footholds on the slope,
no more quakes or volcanic eruptions, floods of tears.
She descends slowly, sure-footed from the cloudburst
of her summit, in no hurry to reach home base.
As she keeps her frail yet firm grip of the rope
on her way down she wonders,
When will it be time to let go?

Sue Cook

A sense of sovereignty where the salmon sing

I climb the mountain of myself to stand
above the cryptic mists that mock the hard-
edged stonecrags and easy couloirs of my
ascent. So high above myself, I stand
outside the frame of everyday regard
that shapes this outward mass.

                              (A raptor cry
shrieks predatory craving from within
the glacial compass of this empty shell,
sends echoes – fast receding – into air
updrafted out beyond where I begin
to see my limit rising on the swell
of turbulence, carried away to…where?)

I climb the mountain of myself and turn
my face away from here. I slew a scree
of sapphic stars against the pressing sky;
each star, a light…each light, a truth yet learned.

Concealed amongst light's shifting shadows, three
answers in moraine: who and what and why?

Janey Mac

Meditating on Gerard Manley Hopkins

In the medieval world
mariners viewed horizons fearfully,
warning on maps, 'Here be monsters'.

Not just sea and land are hazardous,
but Hopkins said it well:
'The mind has mountains…'

I know them well, these mountains,
with their peaks of joy,
their moments of high ecstasy:
a child is born, a book is published,
a lover claims me for his own.
But in the depths, my spirits plummet
to abysses where I know despair.
Blackness descends; I cannot see
how I can make the climb,
the tortuous ascent to happiness again.

Oh yes, these mountains of the mind
are hazardous, with their own monsters.
But I would never choose
the calm and peaceful plains.
I'll take the mountains – with their risks.

Valerie Volk

Holding on

Jamieson Valley, Blue Mountains

Two women in pastel, crimplene skirt-suits,
neglected-cupboard hats and orthopaedic shoes

hasten along the wheelchair-wide clifftop path
holding hands,
       holding on to human.

This wide rushing air,
this canyon of blue and green,
this endless echoing space

terrifies

after so many decades
within cream ward walls.

Gina Mercer

Previously published in *Weaving Nests with Smoke and Stone*,
Walleah Press, 2015

The Moan of the Currawong

She watches the dappled light seep
through the gums to bathe the clinging sedges,
diffuse the shrouds on disconsolate peaks.

The mourning moan of a solitary currawong
transports a hinterland of memories,
cascades through the hidden silence.

The cloudscapes of imagination,
undergrowth of opportunities lost,
the melancholy of grief in all things.

She yearns for the sunlit splash of waterfalls,
exhilaration, the vibrance of invisible heights
amid the weeping rain.

A solace from sadness, she embraces
the muted tremble, the relief of grief,
the misery of mountains.

David Atkinson

The Promised Land

Glasshouse Mountains

You saw them from Sunderland Beach
      on Bribie Island, towering
volcanic plugs of the Glasshouse mountains
said you could see the Himalayas
from your Owl Creek farm
the real journey about to begin.
Were you seeing
the metaphysical 'oneness'
of the glassed-in cross
in its sacred geometry
mirrored in yellowed light
           the cage, in its place, descending
or lifting off
from another dead-end maze?
You said you'd 'found your spot'
among these monoliths

trying to nail something…
before it is lost forever.

Margaret Bradstock

After Lawrence Daws, *Owl Creek Landscape, Glasshouse Mountains*, 1979

Previously published as 'Glasshouse Mountains' in *Barnacle Rock*, Puncher & Wattmann, 2013

Kingfisher

i.m. Deb Westbury (1954–2018)

She's reading – her ear tuned for music
and metaphor, her hand taking the pencil

to the margin. This is the week
the native iris unfolds and wind unfurls

more yellow. In mist over Jamison Valley
Mt Solitary shoulders the early sun.

Cockatoos are specks of paper tracing
a silent path. Trees bunker in the depths,

shrubs hang from the cliff face, their backs
to the warming stone. Two scrub wrens

come close, nimble in their niche.
By the river, she writes, *I saw an azure*

kingfisher snaffle a dragonfly in mid-air.
I thought I even heard the crunch.

Kathryn Fry

Previously published in an earlier form in *Green Point Bearings*, Ginninderra Press, 2018

In the foothills

After all these years I stand in the foothills of self-confidence.
Moments have been when I crested the hill
only to find before me a whole mountain range
stretching ahead to the mists of eternity.

Even on my lowly hill there are dangers:
a thoughtless turn of phrase, a note of sarcasm,
fear of rejection, unreciprocated love
to make me lose my footing on the scree.

Once again and once again, I collect my small achievements,
watch them grow like a snowball till they bear me down
instead of lift me up, and like Sisyphus, I lose the fight
and feel the weight roll over me as we tumble together.

How many times have I reached the summit
only to view the ravine ahead, the sheer cliff face of the next ascent?
Others I know are there, scaling the mountains ahead,
but I know the air is too thin and my skin too thin

to bear the altitudes, the attitudes.
It is safer here in the foothills where the ground is firm
and expectations are light as air. Yet Sisyphus and I
both know the mountain will summon us again.

Margaret Clark

The Hermit

The hermit's gone
on holiday at home
and spends his time
blessing mountaineers.
Fondly suckling
delusions of grandeur,
he sees the pilgrims climb.
But only I,
who have climbed
his holy mountain
so many times
to find him
kissing mirrors,
I who have
scaled his holy mind
so many times
to find it fogbound,
only I can sit back,
thumbs in belt,
and say I still don't know.
That place he goes for safety,
that altar deep inside,
is hard to find
among the clouds
that shroud his mind.

Ian Coulls

Previously published in *Words*, Picaro Poets, Ginninderra Press, 2017, and to be published in *Words, Words, Words: Leaves of Life*, Ginninderra Press

Rock Solid

She found her rhythm
   stood her ground

Rising silently gently slowly
   towards a vast southern sky

Above an ancient land now concealed
Above an ancient ocean unrevealed

Weathered to perfection
Unearthing expression
Often head in the clouds yet wise

Ignoring time completely with its
     peaks of logic
       harshest reasoning
         ridges of emotion
           morphing feeling

She stood her ground
   and found her rhythm

Donna Edwards

There's a shed load of pigs out there

my cousins took me pig hunting *There's a shed load of pigs out there, big ones,* on National Park land, illegal as hell   I was eight   they were twelve and eleven aunts and uncles were in the backyard dark, around the fire pit, not minding us as always, they had tinnies, family grudges, *Schadenfreude*, vindications to hash out

my cousins took their dad's truck, rolled it down the driveway, no noise and no lights rifles wrapped in hessian bags clamped in the back, a big bastard of a spotlight three uncontrollable yellow-eyed pig dogs, berserk with anticipation, skidding around the back-tray   slobber   dog-stink   filthy breath   teeth

mountain gullies, washouts, low scrub, high trees, rotting logs   roaring, bucking, rearing, braking – grunt and squeal of running pigs – chasing boys, curses, yodelling dogs gunshots! in the truck I crouch on the floor, ear on the cadence of the engine, listening for warning coughs and splutters   pressing on the accelerator, to keep the spotlight on

cousins straggle back, already rehearsing the size of the pigs, how many, so close and nearly no blood on their skinning knives, no grunt and heave of a dead pig into the truck tray no scent of death or dying, just the smell of discharged shot, boy bodies sweat, desperate energy, thrilling, running, the chase   stretching, falling, sidestepping, dodging, weaving

afterwards, there was a keeping to the dark edges of the house to avoid a thrashing   boys and dogs and an eight-year-old girl had been where they shouldn't never saw a pig alive or dead, never saw the mountain or the swamp, only the inside of the cabin and a cone of light cutting into nothing

Sandra Renew

Jagged

curved wall   yellow lilies
jagged violet peaks
reflected   intersected
             in the golden glow
i close my eyes   breathe in   *one two three*
breathe out   *four five*
exit anxiety   hello me

i am the mountain
            the mountain is me
battered by rain   buffeted
by wind   seared by sun
i am black wolf   i howl to the moon
above rocky ramparts
      echoes   drum in my heart

i pad with crystal footsteps
stumble   fall   seek answers
eye peaks of wisdom
breathe in   breathe out
conquer mountains
exit anxiety
hello me

Decima Wraxall

Looking Back

As I slowly drove away looking back for the last time
cockatoos flew over stark white against a sombre sky
'SOLD' said the sign on the gate, I was never to return

Living now in the city amongst endless high-rise concrete
stuck in traffic enduring the foul stench of exhaust fumes
sometimes I think of my bush house perched on a hill

I am leaning on the veranda rail winter mist over the lake
seeing mirror images on the water reflected upside down
hearing the calls of birds settling into trees at dusk
In searing summer heat rowing far out in the boat
a forgotten plug, water gushing in, us sinking
frantic barking of the dog drowned out by our laughter

I am walking a dirt track, eucalypt leaves dripping rain
crushing them in my hand, breathing in that pungent odour
while nearby a wombat scurries in fright down a deep hole
Once driving in the dark up a steep track to Mt Terrible
at dawn in silence gazing in awe as the sun rose
casting a soft warm yellow glow over the land below

The new owners built a fence around my bush house
burnt the old deckchairs, they own a shotgun
There is pain in letting go but I can still look back.

Susan-Gaye Anderson

Swiss Alps

The mountains are menacing,
and like sharp teeth,
they eat away at her psyche,
smother, suffocate, close in.

Bathed in terror,
she retreats to recesses of her mind,
seeks refuge, shelter,
to feel safe, find solace.

But the alps threaten,
and oblivious to their majesty,
she panics and cowers
in an avalanche of dread and despair.

She looks up,
and in a low-angle shot,
the peaks loom large, zoom in
and focus on her fear.

Trapped and trembling,
she succumbs to the monsters,
yields to their might as they tower above,
watch over her and reign supreme.

Shelda Rathmann

Questioning heaven

Flying from Mildura after talking with young Joe.
His parents flew me there to help their troubled man.
The pilot shields his eyes from glare of setting sun.

The white of the wing tip reflects a line of silver.
Last gasp sunlight. The awful truth 2 months to go.

The sun sets across a sea of cotton wool cloud
stretching to the finite horizon. Mountains to climb.
The sky above flares up with afterglow.

The Cessna drones on to Adelaide.
The sun has set. I reflect on young Joe's troubles.
Are there cloud bank mountains in heaven?

2 months later his crying father left a phone message,
'Joe hanged himself this morning in the lounge room.'

Is he still discovering those mountain secrets?
20 years after his swift death, we remember him.

Will he greet us when we also mountain climb?

Martin Christmas

Mount Ainslie dreaming

In the clear light above the valley
a snapshot in time
sits framed by the circle of ancient hills
against the blue sky wall of Her gallery
and we embrace
in the warmth of winter coats
against the chill of a Canberra winter
inside a greater truth.

Jennifer Sinclair

Previously published in *Heavenly Seduction and other poems*,
Ginninderra Press, 2018

The Endless Summit

The avalanche
A towering mighty monster
A rocket of snow
Plummeting down
Slippery ice
Hard as a rock
Crash and burn
Locked in a cage
Living in a daze
Thoughts missing
Memory not intact
Hysterical rage
Shivering in the dark
My body shakes and stiffens
Frostbite
Frozen fear
Climbing an endless summit
An ordeal of ruminating cycles
A real delusion
That no one can see
To challenge
The unwanted panic
To begin again.

Jean Winter

'…a circle of blue peaks,
a bowl in which to dip the soul.'

Tony Steven Williams

Namadgi Peaks

The rhythm of pulsing boots
muffled by tussocks,
the track soft and quick,
but memories of huff and puff through
mountain gum and silver wattle
still held in aching calves.

They talk with an easy banter,
loose limbs loping under
a chameleon sky,
jackets sleeved about waists.
The air, cool and pungent,
drips with eucalypt.

Pinched faces meet
the pure, hard wind of the uplands.
Fast clouds drag shadows
across a blur of bush,
a circle of blue peaks,
a bowl in which to dip the soul.

Tony Steven Williams

Namadgi National Park is part of the Australian Alps in the south-west of the ACT.

Previously published in *Close Up & Far Away*, Central Coast Poets anthology, 2000

Flinders Ranges

Steeped in prayer and stooped in thought
these purple-cowled monks
file past in stately cortege
to a compline fixed in time.

They tell their beads in unison,
undercurrents of muffled prayer
that run through mountain ranges
with a rock-strong faith.

Anchored by the gravity of history
layer upon layer washes over them
in a sea of memory that erodes
a grain of sand each day.

They are a silent order.
But when the evening sunlight catches
ancient craggy heads,
all colour sings in deafening praise.

Jill Gloyne

Previously published in *Brushstrokes*, Ginninderra Press, 2017

Caspar David

Moon at dusk
– lambent, full,
filtered through ragged,
leaden clouds.
Man in foreground stands
upon a rugged peak.
He holds a walking staff,
his back towards the viewer.
Gazing at velvet vastness,
streaky lunar yellow,
he almost touches heaven.

Kevin Densley

Previously published in *Tamba*, Number 53, 2013

Tai Shan

The spiritual way starts in darkness,
the climb timed to reach the summit
before the sun breaches the horizon
to shine on roofs of shrine and temple,
catch a flickering of scarlet prayer flags,
slowly reveal ancient sacred cypresses.
The tourist way is by guidebook
minibus and cable car, or meandering
past teahouses and trinket vendors,
making use of frequent selfie stops,
excuses to ease the muscle pains
from thousands of granite steps.
Many emperors took this path,
past the Midway Gate to Heaven
and the Shrine of the Blue Dawn,
through the South Heaven Gate
to the temple at Jade Emperor Peak
for sacrifices and ceremonies.
Confucius once came here
from his nearby home town of Lu,
to gaze at the vistas and cloudscapes
before saying, 'the world is small'.
Mao also climbed to the summit.
What he thought is not recorded.

Mary Jones

Altitude

Faith has more to do
with altitude than attitude.
On the ridge above Machu Picchu
the cadences of the body stills,
each breath its own beatitude.
and our agnostic selves fall away
    like packsaddles
and we can imagine Incan priests
searching omens in the constant shifts of light,
divining truths from rumours of stone on stone.

Roland Leach

a dream of Kunanyi

Mt Wellington, Hobart, Tasmania

to the top of ancient Kunanyi i came
and sailed into the sky
i looked below and saw the sea
as birds went soaring by

from the top of ancient Kunanyi i saw
a world so sweet and new
my heart beat fast in the dream i had
and filled with joy anew

at the top of ancient Kunanyi i felt
my soul rise on the air
it went asearching for my god
who was silently waiting there

Thérèse Corfiatis

Brokenback

The giant dinosaur sleeps
still, unperturbed
nestling the leafy green bowl of rowed vines
within its limbs;
its camouflage coat of grey-brown spotted gum
crested by a spiky backbone
contouring the sky.

Oblivious to the rising drones of cicadas,
totally impervious to the hot heat building, baking,
charging to strobes of lightning
and cracks of thunder
storm washing its sides;
just occasionally cleaning, tidying,
licking its folded skin with warm breath
flaming, flaring, smoke snorting.

It slumbers still. Rock-strong and solid.
Unmoved
for aeons.
Resting –
to rise and greet Him
when we meet Him
in the air.

Adrian Lane

Previously published in *Southpaw*, Ginninderra Press, 2007

Guardians of the Altai

Time pulses fire-red, a sky
distant snow peak blushing
dark/light girdling
flash-dances dreams intent,
encircling mysteries
for eagles orbiting
their do or die
swift-sighted encounters
surfing airs, preying
on fragmented histories
consummating Altai's
forested, timelessly
shiver-white tops soaring,
silver/high lakes blue
mirroring unseen
haunting light breakers,
night/cloud terrors, starred
yet storm wind shakers,
the spirit wakers.

Adrian Rogers

Montacute in winter

my breath a mist
in icy mountain air
celebrating Eucharist
inside the small stone church
every prayer visible

Dawn Colsey

Time Belongim You, Massa

When I opened my eyes again
couldn't see ahead or behind,
looked at my watch – no match for the others' 6th sense
on this mountain – like my laced boots
versus the sandshoe bravado of native boys.
How long will the mist hold me in its grasp?
Then a stone whistled past my ear and I ducked.

Back at the halfway lodge I felt small, cheated,
the Seventh Day Adventist boys having seen the summit
and the sun setting.
'We did it for Sammy, boss,' said Kemsun
stirring the rice and shaving the boiled yam.
Humbled, I smiled at last: 'Is he coming back to Goroka with you?'
'He has to go home to his village. He has payback to settle.
That's why Fat Boy Rasta is here.'
Fat Boy had just rejoined us: superior, all-knowing.
I looked into his eyes. He'd thrown that stone at me, I knew.
'Like us, Sammy wanted to see where God lives first,' Joey added.

Next day the boys went down ahead of me.
Having survived Mount Wilhelm they were proud –
incognisant of my tread again into some sleeping dread.

Danny Gardner

On visiting the Stavrovouni Monastery near Larnaca, Cyprus

We climb the spiral track
six miles above Mesaoria plain
up the Mountain of the Cross
Stavrovouni
Goats scramble
from rock to rock
their bleating in supplication
to the Mystery

Helena mother of Constantine,
brought the Cross
a fragment now in silver
from Jerusalem in three-two-seven
to Aphrodite's realm.
She would not pray there now
women are forbidden
to the Monastery

At the peak
sonorous chimes the bell
as winds whip our hair
while eagles circle down below
and a distant blue Mediterranean
glistens in homage
to the History.

Maureen Mitson

Gunung Batur

there's a lake in a crater next to a dormant volcano
on an island in a tropical sea
and on the edge of this lake the dead are not buried
they lie in the shade of the taru menyan tree

eleven corpses of villagers who died of natural causes
are laid out in their favourite clothes
covered with cages of palm and bamboo
they lie in the shade of the taru menyan tree

the cadavers cannot be burnt in the shadow of the volcano
for fear Ratu Gede Pantjering Djagat will wake and destroy the village
on the lake in the crater on the island in the tropical sea

you can hire a boat to view the bodies
lying on the shore in the shade of the taru menyan tree
and on the return journey the boat will break down
on the lake in the crater next to the silent volcano
on the island in the tropical sea

and to return home, away from those villagers
decomposing on the shore you must pay a small fortune
to hire a new boat on the lake in the crater
next to the slumbering god on his island in the tropical sea

Indrani Perera

Once Were Sacred

We climb the crooked path up Crackenback
to walk the summer's broad palette of flowers:
alpine bluebells, daisies, trigger-plants;
each breath an aspiration, half-formed prayer.

Creamy snow gums, striped with pink and grey,
thick from wrestling wind, curl out of earth.
Flame-breasted robins fire the tussock grass
and ravens rasp the silence with their cries.

Mountains once were sacred, heaven near.
No longer, though: the snow-grass plain is topped
with granite tors awkward in the earth
like broken idols – all that's left of gods.

Feeling some residue of reverence
we hope to cleanse the grime of everyday
in clear, cold air, lifted above it all:
Kosciusko's peak our little ecstasy.

Michael Thorley

'…a mountain reaching for Camelot…'

Sarah Agnew

all aflutter

moth-like, cheeks reach for the sunlight,
eye lids close, breath slows
blood flow and its pump – one breath,
one, time paused, again I
whisper to the Ever Listening *I am here* –
open eyes look, across the Firth,
to the North; head turn to that red
rail icon bridging the Forth;
that fortress rock, the city's chest
puff; twin tower entry to the New
College, older than any where I come
from; the spire for a writer in
a city proud of its writers, with
festivals for its artists; above and away
to the South, the Old, this town, my
home below the tail feather strut
of a mountain reaching for Camelot,
Palace at its feet, and beyond, east,
the sea, the ice-blue sea and on
this hill – the middle of it all –
me, and that unfinished Roman
monument to folly, laughing.

Sarah Agnew

Legend of the Green Domes

These mountains were green domes built by an architect
who spoke in sky and loam and indigenous dialect.
She built them at inception, the first sun almost risen
with care and great reflection on the art of living.
Discovering the essence for making spirit creatures
she added human presence for the domes' safe keeping.
People learned and grew, instructed by the mother.
One day the sacred few were assailed by others
who found a precious stone with an ethereal gleam.
Since all was shared, not owned, the loss was scarcely seen.
Animals and birds no longer could be found.
A roaring noise was heard as the trees came down.
Although the time's not known, I'm sure it was the dawn;
then someone built a throne and poverty was born.

Hazel Hall

Three References to Mountains in Literature

Recent research lets us see
That when Eliot published
In the mountains there you feel free

The right margin stopped him saying
In the mountains there you feel freezing
A rather more pragmatic sentiment

Which occurred to us yesterday in midsummer
Climbing by bicycle from the Derwent
To the sleet-blowing summit of Mt Wellington.

And again, in Katoomba watching demolition work
Bring down the high school with its valley views,
We remember reading mountainous Vergil in a corridor

With legs insensible below the knees
Suggesting the all-too-obvious rhyme *freeze*
And Shelley's famous *trunkless legs of stone.*

John Watson

dunes, perlubie beach

vertebrae honed to a point
backbone's ridge disintegrating
the sharp edge loses focus
drifts off
bleeding into sky

these microboulders rolled
up and over
knife's crest

southern ocean Sisyphus
time's lesson in
persistence

a parable of sand
this relentless wind

air molecules
drum ears and hollows
roar defiance

as sirens beckon sailors

move mountains
a grain at a time.

Rob Walker

Previously published as 'Persistence, Dunes, Perlubie Beach', in *Famous Reporter* #31, and in *micromacro*, Seaview Press, 2006

Valentine's Day 1900

Mount Diogenes (Ngannelong)

The pinnacles, edges of a serrated knife scratch
funereal sky menacing the quiet air.
On two other boulders Hanging Rock teeters,
a jagged scaffold, its ledges protrude,
laid out like etherised tables.

Behind a screen of dogwood and slabs
vertical as tombstones, ferns
grope from fissures, become hands
grappling over moss embossed rock.
You can hide anything here.

Valentine's Day 1900,
schoolgirls mesmerised by heat
clambered up the mountain
in sun's glint. Flash of white
muslin dresses against black boulders

Seen, then gone. Floating ghosts lost.
A frantic search. 'Cooee! Cooee!'
The hollow sound ricocheted
from rocks, echoed around.
No bodies were ever found.

Avril Bradley

This poem references *Picnic at Hanging Rock*, by Joan Lindsay, Cheshire Publishing Ltd, 1967

Among Shadows

Titania Road winds down
from mountain heights to vale
abandoned farms
stretch long and wide

the scene now closing in
pine forests rise to block the sun
as prison teams slash dead-end tracks
and roads are cut by streams

Oberon – a town of winter snow
with men who fish for trout
and women search rain-soaked paths
for mushrooms with exotic names

we journey past Black Springs
no other cars are seen
this all too quiet place
of sheet tin church and graves
held in another time
which never felt at ease.

Michele Fermanis-Winward

Silent Valleys

Morning sun warmed the rocks' old bones,
frost dissolved, bracken steamed
and the mountains ran with waterfalls.
First came the long descent and far below
the forest flowed in waves of silent green,
unpeopled, though every crest seemed
ripe to breed a castle or a kingdom under spell;
European thoughts – mad Ludwig, say,
set down among the blue gums…

Later we took a creek-side path
and found a solitary fish sunning itself
in shallows of moving light.
We climbed again and viewed the valley afresh,
but knew we had no ancient dreaming
to furnish the emptiness. Enough to marvel
as the old explorers must have done,
at a land, so strange and wonderful, yet
so hard to understand, and for us, a second marvel:
all day we had the mountains to ourselves.

Barbara Fisher

The Citadel

That last summer of school, on the beach,
we built a crusader citadel on a mount of sand,
a yard high and six yards round its outer walls,
an Arca, an Ile de Graye, a Crac des Moabites;

Behind the crenellations, a puzzle of lanes,
of flat-roofed houses, crowded souks, medinas,
and at the peak, a basilica, raised upon a synagogue,
destined to be a mosque… It stood for days,

a grand historiography in silica, not even
the local lads pummelled it down. The tide
encircled it, came and went, the wind abraded its
towering expectations, anticipating Babylon.

Christopher Nailer

Haunting Cries

Scotland 2019

Man-made tracks took us to
Snowcapped brooding mountains
Hidden glens
Misted lochs

Whispers of history were heard
In haunting seagull cries
Traditional Gaelic music
That lamented
Heartaches without end

Our stay was brief
Hopefully our footsteps light
On a land and people
Whose past suffering
Cannot be ignored

Brenda Eldridge

Day of Light Festival 299 BC

inspired by the Greek philosopher Epicurus

Being Festival Day
He knew there were throngs
Gathered in the town
And while food was his major passion
Crowds were not
And so, he sat on a small rock on the hill
With valley views to the mountains beyond.

While he savoured these exquisite moments
Quiet contemplation was the exception
As he had many friends
Whom he saw regularly
And though forty-two
Bereft of marriage and wealth
And no doubt a failure to most
In his own eyes
His was a life steeped in riches.

He plucked a golden thread from the dirt
Examined it, while contemplating the long life of the earth
And his passing moment in it
And smiled.

Anthony J. Langford

Mountainous Aspirations

Some mountains aren't yet mountains
Mount Gibraltar an example
    too small to be a mountain
        while hosting a pretentious name
Making a reasonable job
            of being a pretend mountain
    it survives close to its original state
        with an abundance of native trees
            fringing rocky cliff faces
    a muscular glowering presence
        guarding the northern approach to the town
            snuggling into its sheltered valley
These days the Gib displays modest mountain features
    trains humiliated into the innards of a tunnel
        radio signals and similar hampered
            in their arrogant colonisation of the ether
In times past mountains have thrust up outlandishly
        into the welcoming air above
    while discarded others sank from view
One day Mount Gibraltar might look
    from much higher up at the rest of the world
Before then a name change beckons
        Bowrell
    its original Gundungurra title
            ideal

Greg Tome

The Barrier

To the east lies the ocean and, possibly, China.
So no escape that way.
Point in any direction and someone'll tell you.
'Go far enough and you'll find yourself in China.'
The mountains then. Blue across the horizon.
Well, not across the horizon as such.
They're a dreamer's place where known meets notion.
I've heard tell that there're towns beyond. On the other side.
Towns with churches and women in white and carriages in black.
No, not Chinese towns these.
Towns like those I knew before the chains. Where my kin still live.

*

Another grave today. Up above the road. Out of sight behind the gums.
No plaque or headstone. No monument to the road-builder.
The road from where he'd flung himself.
None of us mourned him. Just as we hadn't mourned any of the others.
We fell trees, we break rocks, we build the road, we wear chains.
That's our hand. Our lot.
Following markers blazed by those for whom later monuments will stand.
I waste no concern for them.
Every tree I fell, every rock I break takes me further from Sydney Town.
Closer to those towns beyond.
With churches and women in white and carriages in black.
Or, possibly, China.

Colin Rogers

Red Hands Cave

The mountain track rose
dipped and undulated over rocks
eucalypt branches brushed shoulders
emitting their familiar scent
heat and humidity for companions
till a break through a clearing
the destination – Red Hands Cave.

Cave walls, a gallery
ancient artwork on white talc
hand shapes large and small in ochre
powder blown on to the wall
tourists stood in awe, humbled
honouring artists of the past.

Banksias, scribbly gums and flannel flowers
lined the path back
a rock pool at Campfire Creek
yabbies and dragonflies darted
with insects in afternoon light
before the track led home.

Kay Hefferan

Fame

For some
the road winds slowly
ascending the foothills
to a money-clad mountain peak
and a hacienda mirrored in a glacial lake
until   the black curtain falls.

For others
a long sloping road
rising above startling ballyhoo
ascending to peaks of power
and an eyrie atop a gleaming tower
until   a rival's bid succeeds.

And for a few
a circling road
rising upward, stepping forward then sliding back
persisting to reach a snow-clad summit
admired by millions across the plains
forever etched   on history's page.

Geoff Graetz

'I cannot speak rainforest or cloud
nor walk mountain paths.
Language slips from me.
There is no sound here.'

Anne Kellas

birdwing

kunanyi (Mt Wellington)

Birdwing
glimpsed in a watercolour sky
– white
turns into winter mist.

Soft rain
on the grey mountainside
slides
in a lessening of less.

Bare stalks of trees near the summit
lean at an angle in the gale.
Time's a soft tissue injury
a rift.

Threads broken
in the blanket weave of leaves.
A vague purple shade of green
seeps into the dark.

I cannot speak rainforest or cloud
nor walk mountain paths.
Language slips from me.
There is no sound here.

Anne Kellas

Previously published online as 'kunanyi/Mt Wellington' as one of three highly commended poems in the 2018 Bruce Dawe National Poetry Prize

Descendings

Your eyes, when I think of them, looking down from
the high country into the hunkered valleys, had that
hanker and focus for some sure hold on life; like when
I was ten and looked down the steep run of the street
from my box cart as if I could have been descending Everest,
except for the neighbours carrying their shopping back home,
whom I had to steer around with all strength and grip
to keep the axle steady, hurtling perilously close, their pale,
shocked looks in my periphery. With the same bearing
towards trial and self-belief against all the forces pulling,
you would have stayed up there happy on heath and scrub,
reborn amongst the vast farnesses where you always saw
yourself, remote, but ardent again, all sense for all else gone;
everything there unmoving, the long makings of height
fixed firm into the ground set with steeps and plummets,
interlocked, like wheel and counter-wheel, the whole land
stilled and balanced against itself. What was more alone
then, that place, or you in that place? Time slows, they say,
as you get higher, as if there are always strange workings
to the mechanisms of the world. As we descended, slowly,
our lives speeding up again, drawing on us, you looked
back up, a mountain-homing revenant, your eyes clinging
to a sense of lag, something of you time-caught
on those crag-toothed heights, and never coming down.

Philip Radmall

Pink Champagne in the Blue Mountains

Call of lyre, crackle of twig
Dragon breath of eucalypt
Misty hair dewdropped with cloud
Cooee of a distant child

Solo trek
Pace of heart
Mind in flight
Silent art

Pause on precipice
Arc valley stone
And another for those
Who've left us alone

Ahh, ahh, all alone…
Echoes the falling stone, with crow in harmony above.
Blue Mountain whispers (ancient wise)
'Raise a toast for all goodbyes. Pink champagne for loss my love.'

Ghost gum beckons earthly embrace
In sympathy with the human race
'Shhh shh share your cries…
Everyone dies…everyone dies…'

Melissa Bruce

Novice retreats: day 1

High above nunnery, rock outcrop, crumbling edges, deep drops.
Stoop under bluff overhang, duck head, enter mouth.
Smell of dampness, air cooler, ever greyer till blackened crawl space beyond.
Uneven ground, candle stub on scrap of tin touching reed mat.
Torchlight on wall of Buddhas, scenes from sacred texts, monitor lizard – all teeth and muscle
Cobra arching hood, hand-sized scorpions, spiders and rats.
Crevices and ledges of animal droppings, webs hung in insect husks.
Tarantula emerges high on hairy legs spread like fingers.
Throat tightens, tears form.
In none of her dreams was the cave as small and ugly as this one.
She thought of herself, passing the seasons, how she would cope.
Abbess: *Remember, though not as young, they all felt the same fears you'll be feeling.*
Drops pack, retreats outside to absolute silence, like that in deep space.
Sits on rock shelf level with distant summits, draws in legs, meditates
Till thunder fills her ears, lightning her sight, rain her robe and skin.
Cups her hands and drinks from water streaming down the cave mouth
Till the storm passes and she disrobes, sun beaming down on shoulders, belly and legs
Warmed through and through, takes rest of the day to write –
After the deluge
Trees emerge as sun-touched glass,
Puffs of mist rising.
All the world wet and warm.
God light gleaming over me.
Abbess: *Thought thrives best in solitude.*
And it did.

Steve Tolb

this new moon

props its lopsided smile
on the rugged horizon

in the silent mountains
one rock tumbles creekwards

darkness blows away

moonlit ridges of under-leaf
frame cliff faces

there's a roguish glint
in Earth's molybdenum eye

Tim Metcalf

Previously published in *Into the No Zone*, Ginninderra Press, 2003

You Yangs

for Patrick

Startling aberration sprawling on the edge of that flat plain,
mystically looming, like an arm's length Hanging Rock

He loved the name, *it had to mean something significant*
to the local Wathaurong, had to be a creation tale, a fallen star

pushed out of heaven and turned into an ugly lump,
an Icarus star, punished for flying too high…

He was disappointed then amused, to find it meant
big hill in the middle of plain

Mathew Flinders climbed it first, on May first
Your birthday! We should climb it on your birthday…

Of course, his insatiable embrace, see a mountain
be a goat, see an ocean, be a fish. *Drink it in through your skin*

You Yangs – symbol now of expectations crushed, promise unfulfilled,
sulking there on that flat plain – hunkering into solitude

Karen Throssell

The You Yangs are a small mountain range situated on the Geelong Plain in Victoria.

After she left

She sits with a gin and tonic on the deck of her life
precisely alone except for the landscape
with its pockets of sound and the mountain
opposite watching

She studies its stillness its shadow and edge
knows how something so big can be so quietly there

She imagines it breathing treetops dancing its rhythm

J V Birch

Previously published in *Our Voice*, Australia, 2016

Alone between sentences

Making mountains from molehills
an art she's perfected
only one of her problems
they say
waving their paper diplomas like
entitlement banners

proclamations before
other homes fostered with
the same 'fathers'
as her own home-grown one
juvenile correction

and later appearing
before courts
convictions incarceration
and isolation cells
solitary confinement
although she's
always been
alone between sentences

Myra King

Cloud Dreaming

from a journey   forty years back
a mountain cloud dreaming   like breath held

so it lives where I live
with poems of precious things

my house of wood   breathes with the wind
and life slips into place as it should

parrots   echoes of memory   seek seeds
among the leaf patterns in the grass

in my garden blue iris rise among the stones
dreaming clouds unravel a shimmering blue mist

night birds   wings drifting
toward lines of loneliness

Lorna Thrift Brooks

The Wedge-tailed Eagle

High above the mixture of mist and rocks,
He is the silent assassin,
Come to collude with the mountain's early wind,
Quarter the dry-lipped gullies,
Sketch his shadow on the scoured rocks,
Turn to erase all sign of his passing
And swing clear, with never a tremble of his wings.
He will fall, silent and brown between the cliffs,
To crack the skull of a fox
Or bury his butcher beak in the belly of a slaughtered deer,
Then lift into the rasping wind,
Bloodied, but satisfied and heavy-laden.
He will snatch any unwary rabbit,
Feed it to two or three semi-bald heads
That stick out, bulbous-eyed,
From the rough bomb blast of his nest.
Then, with the sun spilling copper through the gorge,
He will launch himself back into the wind,
The silent assassin once more on patrol.

William Cotter

Thinking Like a Mountain

The mountain moves through stillness,
a force with no velocity,
a power without motion.
Known by many names, it changes
with the season, with the observer.
Born in fiery chaos,
it reinvents itself over and over,
yet is immutable, a constant.
Only the mountain sees all.
An anchor, in its pathos, harmony and memory,
it has the hardness of reality,
yet it reflects the wild thing within us that would possess us.
I sleep,
yet the mountain already sees the dawn alight.

John Weerden

alone unknown

Thrust upward from the gentle earth
The even greens the hollyhocks
The sloping flanks begin their climb
Of hidden copses   needled pines
That scent the paths that have no end
The larkspur and the song of larks
The whispers and the restful earth
Change shape
Thrust skyward
Monuments
of creviced rock
a darting hare   a hissing snake
a bush that pushes
through a crack
Layers of layers pack   impact
Grey and brown   cream and black
Sprinkles of sparkle caught in light
on rocks that strain   bathed by rain
The upward climb   the unkind wind
Thrust onward now
toward the brow
scaled and bald
the hoary head
sleeps weary worn
among the dead

Maureen Mendelowitz

Rosebery, West Coast, Tasmania

My father thought I was a 'nance'
For singing in a church choir dressed
In cassock, surplice, lizard frill,
My mother chased me with his belt

And screamed 'you little bugger' as
We went. My brother was my foe,
And when my sister's coming turned
My love, forbidden, into hate,

Mount Black, so close our lawn was dark
And wet all year, confirmed my need
To hug shadows, see on nearby
Sombrely grey, deceptively –

Sometimes-sunlit, Mount Murchison,
A face resembling mine, to which
I felt welcomed to give my lone,
Unforgiving, cold hardened heart.

Graeme Hetherington

Our place

A specific quietness.
A mountain.
Windows thinly iced each morning.

That was ours alone.

A cola-coloured river.
Old objects restored
to brand-new oldness.

That was ours alone.

Temperate rainforest.
Moss and lichen.
Everything mollified by foliage.

That was ours alone.

Us inseparable,
as if it couldn't end.

That was ours alone.

Mark Mahemoff

Coachwood Glen

Silence, almost silence.
The creek trickles,
hairs of a bow vibrating on rock.
The looming roughness of the cliff above
glows between cracks in the leaves.

Silence, then a chime,
warm and embodied,
three notes playfully repeating.
My gasp rises –

So sudden in swiftness,
it lands on a log.
Feathers ruffle,
darting beak preens.

Black eyes glint
from a yellow stripe,
another lands, then another,
the first shoots up to the leaves.

Silence, moistness,
translucent canopy –
I wait again for song.

Charles Freyberg

'But for now, all my future was marls and crags shales and clays, the thin bed of dark pebbles full of sharks' teeth high on the cliff face…'

Christopher Palmer

The view from below

We'd drive for hours, quiet spectators
of landscapes boasting in green
towns in their slow cycle of ruin and renewal
and villages no more than a car length
with their otherworldly names: Ravenscar,
Llantwit Major, Druidston Haven.

     Pick-up time arranged, you'd leave me
to a boy's growing sense of the day; no plan
but an urgency reaching down to low tide
as far as the headland, filling my nose and clothes and hair
with the scent of iron, damp sand and salt; and later the house
when I'd empty bag loads onto the kitchen table
for analysis and baking in the oven.

     But for now, all my future was marls and crags
shales and clays, the thin bed of dark pebbles
full of sharks' teeth high on the cliff face, revealed
with chisels, picks, and a lack of fear;
like the horses we'd see along the way
etched into existence, whiter than bone.

     Zigzagging the intertidal, I'd chase signatures
of the long-absent, until teased by seaweed, showered in foam.
Then you'd return, a sudden foreground
in the eroded afternoon, lost to time
and I'd look up from a bed of my own footprints
to layers I could see but never reach.

Christopher Palmer

Previously published in *The Galway Review*, March 2019

Because it's there

Everest's call-up came again, insistent.
You, still yearning, still eager for the quest,
took along champagne, 60 cans of foie gras,
The Complete Works.
Photos of you formal with the chaps,
don't show the sheer plod and haul in store.
To your wife you wrote
I cannot tell you how it possesses me.
And still it does.

Seven decades on, searchers see *A patch of white. It wasn't snow*,
find you face down, embracing Mother Goddess of the World.
The wind has stripped protection from your back,
still broad and strong, but *matte like marble*.
Bits of hobnailed boot, some sock, a rope around your waist,
enough of your clothes to see the pattern of your tweed,
and a name tag: *George Mallory.*
A watch – now faceless, timeless, but not the photo of your wife
you promised to plant on the summit.
Did you make it to the mountaintop?
Were you on your way home?
No prayer flags flutter for you,
just a shred of reddish hair stiff in the bitter wind.

Marg Collett

Rock and Sky

leaves the trees and falters before the plunge of sky and horizon. Looks around. Can't ignore the tightness in his chest, the tug at his stomach drawing him to the edge. Takes another step, the grass threadbare on granite, beyond gathering. Then another. Digs toes of his boots into any crack in rock. Worries a tuft of grass may trip him. Shuffles forward, bends knees, presents a smaller target to the attraction of air beyond the edge.

He goes to all fours. On either side, nothing but air. Does not look up, does not look down. Has left the grass behind him. Feels the abrasive impediment of stone and flint chip to the weight of him as he crawls. Lowers his chest, fearful a sudden rush of wind will lift him from the mountain and spill him to the matted bush below, or hurl him so far into the inflamed sky he will never know earth again. Inch, inch, slow arresting inch along the jutting outcrop, exhilaration of mountain.

Straddles the slim knob of rock. Legs dangle. Muscles and nerves quiver. Drops ever so slightly between the gusts of testing wind. Mere inches away from the final edge, he can peer into space on either side of him by the slightest turn of his head, barest flicker of eye movement. Sees the broken boundary of mountain, scoring by wind and sporadic storm, struggle of plant and bird nest, slew of cliff to teeming vegetation, but cannot see beyond that final edge. Hands grip rock. Thighs grip rock. Body desires to be rock as it hunches. Feet tremble like the ends of a tuning fork.

Moments away from falling, from flying, from knowing what to dare.

His face to the sun, throat open to air.

Earl Livings

dolloped out there

islands, three, dolloped out there,
silent on horizon, hint of bend where
yes, you walked one, bled on one, once

flinty and hard as truth,
Michaelmas, Breaksea, Mistaken,
three islands, dolloped out there

barefooted, late autumn, off the
dinghy, all map and scheme, blind to sense,
you bled on one, walked one, once

remainders, middle pinned by lighthouse,
eye closed over now, drab reminders
dolloped out there, islands, three

'twas rock and hell's arc of scree,
at the unseen tip, in Southern's wash
you walking, you bleeding, once

half round, turned back, spume and swell, soles
gashed by shell, by granite, one gull in watch
at you walking, bleeding, back, on one of
three, islands, dolloped out there

Kevin Gillam

Tour de France

The peloton, a multicoloured ribbon,
surges across the landscape,
riders' concentration set
hard as their saddles,
their movement,
fluid as a fish's tail.
Country coded,
muscle primed and flying,
they transform their fatigue
into ripped determination.
It propels them
across soft velvet folds
of meadow and mountain,
a swaying paintbox.
Occasionally a spill
disfigures the canvas
but mechanically they reform
and flow on like textile,
a sarong wrapping the road,
a pulsating tapestry.
Then holes appear
and the fabric begins to unravel
in the sprint for the line
where heads lift
and pumped fists telegraph victory.

Fran Graham

Mount Field Shadows

Explore the undergrowth
life at the bottom is rich, bosky-damp
the lime light soothes
as you awaken to oxygen's kiss.
Photos by the fallen swamp gum
mark your fairy size. Velvet-moss tangle, tree-fern giants
confide in riffle creek companion.
Tourists read the signs
huddle on the bridge revived
by the cataract's drifting spray.
Potoroos scurry into the bower
behind picture-pretty myrtle and long-legged laurel.
Nearby a platypus hides in the gurgle
as the faintest shadow of yourself
moves ahead on the path.

Anne Collins

Previously published in *Poet-Tree 2008* and in *My Friends This Landscape*, Ginninderra Press, 2011

Waiting for Baby

I've done this waiting before, on a mountain
Ten thousand feet, despairing
For that vital break in the weather
Rolling cigarettes, making another brew
Reading Emily Dickinson, rucksack packed
Retying prusik loops, adjusting crampon straps
In a smoky festering hut
Until ten days later the hogsbacks break a moment after midnight
Out and up, headlamps umbilical rope, first slot opens
Between rock and ice, belays over snowbridge
Last two hundred only pain no strength remains in arms legs
Cramps
Summit
Before dawn

Sack packed again, waiting
Reading Emily Dickinson after all these years
No cigarettes, making a brew only a few days to go
Hold on for a break in the weather
Another brew in a clean warm house
Until ten days later the waters break, monitor's out, heartbeat's up
Last two hundred only pain some strength remains in arms legs
Contractions
Birth
Before dawn

Richard Stanton

Intrusion

I am Eiger, Alp Mountain,
the one with the North Wall,
notorious,
who has claimed many foolhardy men,
too arrogant to climb my easy flanks.

I have no compassion for those
who scale us tall beauties,
like frenetic ants,
no respect.
If only we, the tallest of the tall,
could find a less brutal way
to keep climbers at bay,
those, like Hilary on my friend Everest:
'We knocked the bastard off.'
Tenzing – bless him – prayed
to the Gods, scattered his orisons.

Everest, stunned by the invasion
of humanity's boots,
never the same.

Alice Shore

Gibraltar Ranges Ramble

A whiff of campfire smoke lingers
as fingers warmed by steaming coffee thaw.
Shivers of winter sun glance through stringy bark,
tremble on lace-leafed wattles and
tingle the tips of scrawny banksias.
A perfect morning for a ramble
through summer torched forest.

Blackened trunks of grass-trees stalk the hillside,
their bright new headdresses shimmering
amongst soft epicormal growth of gums –
survivors in an ever-harsher land.

Emerging into a sunny clearing,
where scorched earth has washed away
exposing crusted granite outcrops,
our track is cut by a sunning python
slowly digesting the bulge in his middle.
He watches, immobile. We skirt him, respectfully
and in the distance the rumble of tumbling water
announces a stream bouncing to the valley.
Honeyeaters feasting on cliff-hanging blossom
dare us to step closer and look down.

Jacqui Merckenschlager

Crossing the Alps

All day we raced across the plains of northern Italy
in the rain. We saw grey stone farmhouses off
in the distance, hunched protectively around
central courtyards, and tall, thin, leafless poplars,
in endless rows. By late afternoon, we came
to the mountains, blanketed in heavy mist.
We rose up through the mist, like flying through cloud –
an atmosphere weightless, placeless, suspended in
a cold, grey aether. Then, right on sunset, the clouds
parted to afford a sudden view of snow-clad peaks,
bathed in hues of gold and orange and pink, a sugary
confection at the top of the world. Rain closed in again
and took us away, down the French side of the Alps,
past Turneresque scenes of gigantic destruction – avalanches
stopped, heart-thrillingly, metres from tiny villages
that clung to impossibly steep slopes, glimpsed in gaps
between the clouds, through the gathering gloom of dusk –
and on into the blackness of the southern French night.

Stephen Smithyman

Pauline Hanson's Bumslide Downward

The iconic mountainous
height – to climb or not
to climb? Those here
before us whitefellas,
say no, and whether
they're asking or telling
us not to, isn't really
the point, is it? Because
when the name changed,
from Ayers Rock, to Uluru,
surely that rock became
unclimbable, didn't it?

Carolyn Cordon

Cresting the Peak

Less than two hundred metres from cresting the peak
I surrendered to stone lying drenched in the shade.
Far below to my left and my right and before me
in tortuous gorges the tree martins played.

There those tiny hang-gliders arrested and bound me
extracting the essence from every breeze
which, exhausted like I was, still summoned the power
to carry the songs being sung by the trees.

Where the needle-like limbs of each green Xanthorrhoea
embedded as firmly as rock in the ground
waved as innocently as anemone tendrils
attracting a meal in some liquid surround.

While above me, still climbing with fierce resolution
were three from my party, a refracted line
and on reaching the summit, their mission accomplished
they soaked in the view that, perhaps, could be mine.

Yet below them I leisurely drank from the grandeur
of *less* than their 'hundred per cent' summit view.
But although I'll float dreams of the day I may join them
my ninety per center will just as well do.

Max Merckenschlager

Endings

at the end of
the longest
staircase
of stars –
there will be
mornings
when our hearts are
small birds
with clipped wings
and
each truth
we keep
is a vase without
a single flower
and
our hands
are idle paper
yachts –
on an ocean of skin

Jules Leigh Koch

'The mountain becomes a shadow
of its former self wrapped in a cloak of mystery…'

ML Grace

Winter Shroud

The mountain becomes a shadow
of its former self wrapped in a cloak of mystery
while wombats dig deeper to await
the first welcoming of snow melt
with the scent of forthcoming spring
and the smell of diesel from chairlifts

Snow falls silently in the early light.
Creeps in, as a fox after prey, swirling
white goose feathers that thicken,
to dust the snow gums with the plucking,
spreading a blanket of white over
huge unmovable black boulders.

A cruel metal blue sky tangles cloud
into clefts, secreting the valley depths
with purple shadow wrapped in fog.
Listen to the black crows in raucous
discussion of what the day may hold
in the way of food and shelter.

Standing on the white ridge top
this hidden power of the mountain
becomes palpable and the world below,
                insignificant.

ML Grace

Tar-Neem-Er-Ra

My eyes trace her chiselled face
her rocky façade sculptured by Time
and worn by winds from the west
she rests against the eastern escarpment
her forested skirt flows
into those of two western sisters
shielding sites once sacred to women:
first females chipped ochre here
shared stories   taught lore   birthed new generations
danced and sang the joy   and sadness of living.
From meandering creek   to hidden caves
this land contains memories of
graves of babes born   too delicate to survive;
celebrations   of womanhood attained;
the shared witnessing   of the wisdom of elders.

Newcomers came   altered the cloak of her slopes;
named the lofty trinity: Roland, Claude, Van Dyke.

As I walk the valley track below her peak
treading reverently in awe of her mystery
and secrets held there throughout history
one sorrowful word wafts on the breeze
whispering through branches of ancient trees:
> *Tar-Neem-Er-Ra.*

Dianne Kennedy

To some of the old people, land to the south of their country, including the mountains, was known as Tar-Neem-Er-Ra (big grassy plains).

...sters' Redress

...mping frilled lichens to death
...boys pounded up the squelching track,
...tting the gutsy rhizomes of incautious bracken
...d scoring bare-breasted mountain ash with scissored initials.
...eir Hansel and Gretel wake glistened with ripped chip and choc packs.

...the clearing, they peeled back the view of the valley below with their eyes
...d plunged their iron poles into the gentle heart of the earth.
...e smoke and stench of their meat and blood fizzing on hotplates
...ralled ghostly against the purple air.
...ey devoured and drank and spat and blitzed the forest with profanities
...t glued them together
...inst their fear
...he night bore down
...d the sorority of trees sighed to one another like wronged sisters.

...ey huddled separately underneath the canopy as stars winked,
...d shielded their ears from the boobook lament and dreadful stirring-chirring nightjar.

...uzy, crusty ice, freshly strewn on the alpine flesh, flashed at the dawn procession.

...king away the brilliant snow and nests of trash
...searchers lowered their heads and babbled freak storm into their black phones
...hey rolled back the petrified human logs.

Jane Carmody

Two-faced

Janus of the mountains
You are my friend and foe
Your roads a winding welcome
To turn the pages
In a living wilderness calendar.
Vistas and valleys
Wonderland of hues and shadows
Your outstretched ranges reach out
Inviting me to explore.
Dappled sun or slicing rain,
Capriciously you catch and divert.
And when you have me nestled on the slopes
Lulled by a lyrical waterfall
Seduced by towering eucalypts or spiralled ferns
Then you turn.
Warning smell of smoke awakens my nostrils
Vivid crimson glow crowns your bushy head
Roaring wind becomes your siren song
You fling hot embers that dance and fly,
Lethal tasters of the coming flames.
I feel the heat
As I see your other face.

Jeanette Woods

As I Air Punch

There are no more superlatives –
and from computer modes mere crystal-ball games
you search for models but you'll never find my range

Air punch clouds to sharpen as I rake all round the world
I am nature's invisible keeper – cut in rock, granite & stone.
And *your* mud maps & *my* terrain is severed, as you ply me with pretty names
like *Agung, Olympus, Baldy* and *Everest*; and the list goes on and on and on.
Do you feel my temper scorching where your indifferences nail you to your walls;
though my vengeful rakes came knocking; to deaf ears blind eyes and your yawns!
And I'm done with your blind laws and damned biases;
your looped policies of plagued paperchains – that you hang out with fake-news disclaimers;
they're loopy-loops going round and around – again and again –
now! – you panic with lame prayers to bent knees; those self-selfies – well-looped and worn;
your kismet I've chewed up and spat out when my thunderclap knocked on your doors.
And your backs are so busy yawning – though the obvious is patent and dour,
I face you with raised shoulders aching but *your yawns* grow louder grow dire.
Alas! your turned backs look so familiar as I rake all round the world;
I am nature's invisible keeper – cut in rock, granite & stone.

David Taylor

Tonight the Monaro storm comes from the south

She hides in dark skirts
her bronze drought thighs
just out of sight
over the hills
golden breasts swell
in unselfconscious show
of round and pale cleavage
the ranges reveal
trees white limbs stripped naked
to lipstick-red bark
hang from forks
in pleated folds
pink flower heads
dance in wind's choreography
taunt just out of touch
in sky-stopped air
heavy with breathing
redolent with anticipation
a sudden flash of lightning's fury
disconcerting
as the night in Limehouse
after dinner in Soho.

Peter Hansen

Plain old rock cake

Cape Town 1972

Every city should have a Table Mountain
looking down on it, putting it in its place.
Take nothing for granted, it says. I am bigger, stronger.
I'll still be here long after Mother Earth has taken
you back and wound you round with weeds.

Katoomba 1992

The Three Sisters are out there somewhere,
cloaked head-to-foot in Blue Mountain mist –
like the Brontes chasing chapter, line and verse
out on the moors. Catching their death.

Canberra 2019

Today, the city's Brindabella backdrop glints
white in the sun. Snow runs down its upper slopes
like icing on a cake still warm from the oven.
In a day or two, we'll be buttering up
to plain old rock cake again.

Louise Nicholas

In the High Country

On the snowline a scramble of gums
trunks rinsed with the memory of blood,
prepares for another bout with the tyranny of weather.
Today's a truce. Quiet as the poison farmers
pushed deep into the earth.
Quiet as a billy button's yellow fist,
a pugilist's whispered threat or the hush of snow.
Quiet as a pygmy possum in the whorled palm of my hand.

I think of explorations: men with maps wrapped in pigskin,
din of shovel, thud of pick – the rush of miners to claim
colour under a lunatic sky. A crow calls below.
Thredbo looks like a toy town guarded by an anxious child
waiting for the school bully to pounce,
knock him down and jump on it.

Moya Pacey

Previously published in *The Wardrobe*, Ginninderra Press, 2009

A Great Ungreen

Mount Tennent, 2003

An eagle east from Ingledene
sails close to climb up cliff and cloud.
It ghosts the grave and gaunt ungreen,
its shadow shears the ash-grey shroud.

Here Fire flared and flailed its fists
and wrenched the roots and rocks around.
In spots its seething still persists
like demons deep in darkness drowned.

I tread a track through tortured trees,
their branches brand me black and bleed,
erasing relished reveries
when Tennent towered teal-green-treed.

Were Heydrich's hitmen harboured here,
so strong the sense of scorch and sand?
And yet some yeast of yesteryear
lies light like lint along this land.

A silent song of scents dispersed
impels these pale impacted plants
to thrive and thread through thorns and thirst
and shed their sloughs of circumstance.

Maurits Zwankhuizen

Sublime Point

I stood on a white cloud sea,
the rising sun projecting me
on a ghostly screen
in the chasm below.

A halo of rainbow hue
formed around my silhouette
which grew until, cloud ascending,
the image was consumed in vapour.

Three black cockatoos floated past
with funereal cry
as I and all the solid world
were drowned in white oblivion.

Now my haloed shape re-formed,
I moved my arms like a great bird.
They were angel wings
in time-lapse photography

until a cold mist enveloped me
and my rock, entirely.
Eyes closed, I breathed in the dawn
of a world born anew.

Brendan Doyle

Previously published in *The Wooden Gate*, Ginninderra Press, 2017

Silk Road

Tien Shan Mountains

So close I could touch you
from this oval window.
Standing together as a crowd
in uneven rows, jostling
your united front a barrier
for nomads, traders, pilgrims.
It is late summer. Your ermine cloak
has worn thin and slipped
baring dark angular shoulders
rocks and screes devoid of plants
sharply sloping into mysterious depths.
Faxian in 400 told of a poison dragon
there, with power to blind a man
or make him froth and die.

Jean McArthur

Watagan Walk

There was a moment, Mount Warrawolong in view
throat constricted with the effort of climbing
where I stopped thinking about you.

Only fools would work this hard I heard you say
but it was just wind in my ears, clouds parting briefly
for a shot of blue, past boulders covered in moss, Illawarra flame
red cedar branches, walking barefoot, my feet treading
lightly on broken promises, like the memory of kinship
wedge-tailed eagle overhead, eyes squinting against summer sun.

How easy it would be to reject this gift that was never mine
city girl on the hill, plastic sunnies and khaki lips
whiter than ice cream mountain tops.

Yet I call this forest home, find my own handprint
in abandoned caves, recognise goannas blending to bark
the screech of lorikeet and cockatoo
more familiar than a honking horn

Eucalyptus breath draws me back
as if it were a return c'mon it says
your body is earthbound this soil, this smell.

Magdalena Ball

Previously published in an earlier form in *Unmaking Atoms*,
Ginninderra Press, 2017

In Summer's Heat

Blue Mountains, NSW

Who has taken up this azure veil,
casting it like a mantle
to float silently into the valleys,
to tangle with trees,
to drift over rugged peaks and cliffs,
escarpments and chasms
and then away, away into the distance
as far as the eye can see?
As the vivid mist rises,
the colour of lapis lazuli,
its earthy opulence carries
the essence of the eucalypt.
And who, enveloped in summer's heat,
savouring the heady aroma
and gazing over these mountains
has not stood, caught in awe,
and wondered at this infinite mystery?

Elaine Barker

My Milky Way

for Eric, Linda and Louise

Last year we walked
on the rim of the Blue Mountains
from Gordon Falls to Leura Cascades.
As far as the eye could see
the green of a thousand trees
met the blue of a limitless sky,
ancient escarpments kissed by the sun,
the Bridal Veil Falls shivered silver, white.
Today below and above every lookout
thick misty-white fog
like a giant cloud fills the valley.
If someone said the end of the world has come,
if someone said the Milky Way is visiting
the Blue Mountains, I'd say wonders never cease.
'Look up,' one of you whispered,
'it's like a Chinese painting.'
Branches merge with mist.
Clothed in fine silk, silver leaves
on invisible threads hang from the heavens.
Twigs like pencil marks on a draftsman's page
pale-grey light-green fade into whiteness.

Maurice Whelan

Previously published in an earlier form under the title of 'Magic Mountain' in *Excalibur's Return*, Ginninderra Press, 2011

Giant Stinging Trees

Tamborine Mountain

Most unapproachable of trees, their highnesses
and majesties, hostile to human travellers
who trespass on their territory, are in command
of glassy armouries: cilia on surfaces
of stems and leaves that target skin,
a company of archers whose unerring barbs
drive their victims half insane with agony.

Beware the lofty ogres of the rainforest,
grim guardians whose dark fruit proves
benign to just a favoured few – green catbirds,
regent bowerbirds; skeletal vestiges of leaves
bear witness to the appetites of leaf beetles.

Insidious and instant shock
impact of these hermetic beings –
the neurotoxin sealed in silicon –
fascinates warmongers with its wizardry.
It's claimed the toxin of such trees
stays potent for a century, each hair a vial
of utmost pain, nature's torture without balm,
for if there is an anodyne, we've yet to learn its name.

Jena Woodhouse

Previously published in *Green Dance: Tamborine Mountain Poems*, Calanthe Press, 2018

Aloof

Mount Remarkable

With her head in the clouds
does she notice her feet?

Is she aware of the criss-crossed paths?
The scores of riders
hurtling down at breakneck speeds?

In her dignified winter dress
– great coat of forest green
buttons of granite scree –
she appears haughty and indifferent.

But
I notice how
she shrugs her shoulders
nudges a cloud over her peak.

And, as it unleashes its load
on those adrenalin seekers
splashing mud up their backsides

only I see her
snigger.

Kristin Martin

Pursuing

Untamed towering flame
of leaping orange
roars up timber   jumps chasms
fills canyons with trapped smoke
squeezing air from homes and lungs

hot-poker anger
ignites   crackles   snaps
moves across kunanyi's body
red and new
ready to kill

unheeding of damp skies
flaring and trembling
might combusts
and explodes
till there is no more

like a flash eclipse
unreasonably   morbidly
black ash smoulders
dying and cool
the lack of human kind

or nature's way of rekindling

Elizabeth Goodsir

Wellington Moods

Mount Wellington,
part of our lives, dominating the views
of Hobart, homes, and the conversations of the weather-conscious:
'Mountain's clear – fine today.'
The hour, weather, seasons, control its emotions
light and shadow flicker like expressions across its face.

In the harsh summer sun, it is an ancient countenance,
grey and dry, full of character with the scars of its Ages.
In autumn, sunrises spotlight it, gold, red
radiant above the silhouetted town.

In winter, it broods darkly, under snow clouds,
lifting to reveal a brilliant white mask. Spectacular.
In spring, the sun shines softly, kindly, so that it appears opaque
blue, patterned with wisps of white cloud, trailing like elusive veils.

At night, black, monstrous, it crouches, primeval,
against a starlit sky, new moon glowing.
Sometimes it tires of the show, the constant watching. Then it draws low
a heavy screen of cloud.

It is as if it has never been, and its absence puzzles tourists passing through.
They have heard that Mount Wellington dominates the Hobart scene.

Judith E.P. Johnson

Previously published in an earlier form under the title 'Mountain Moods' in
The Mercury, 1987, *Mountain Moods*, VDL, 1997 and in *Landmarks*,
Ginninderra Press, 2005

Perspectives

At dawn, there is a softness to the mountains;
muting the crags and cliffs
that fall precipitously to valleys;
shadowed and inaccessible.
Mysterious.

Panoramas that ache
for captured images on phone or ipad;
or perhaps a retro SLR with many lenses
hanging from an obsessed amateur.
Obscured by fog.

A gash of highway cuts this mountain barrier,
leaving a keloid of strip development.
Fast food and boutique antiquities (New Age).
Yet all around nature's energy threatens
immolation.

As the mist clears
a blue-tinted immensity
reaches out to our primal senses
and leaves us speechless.

Mark d'Arbon

Eagle on High

Mt Kosciuszko

Water tumbles over stones beneath pygmy possum's paws
After a glance at the sky, it scrambles to safety

Far off, above the windblown slopes
a wedge-tailed eagle watches the marsupial disappear
The hungry eagle drops
then rises
barely moving its elegant wings
waiting patiently
It flies across scrubby mountain top
down into the valley,
lands on a solitary snow gum
sits motionless
a snake warms its belly on the roadside
Sensing footsteps, slithers beneath the concrete walkway

A human tide strides up a convenient metal platform
The height needs conquering
Achievement will be cherished
Few notice puddles left by last night's rain
Fewer admire yellow dots of the billy button flowers
One lifts their eyes and watches the eagle soar once more

Barbara Gurney

Bush Trance

sixteen ks of dirt road and the map leaves me unprepared
for the depth and extent of pots ripples and dents
baked fossilised mud of rain wash-off from last autumn's drench
I'd turn back if I could find a turning place
I go into that bush trance paradox
this old place winding the tension out of my neck
as I worry about upcoming suspension repairs
this old place working its dreaming
while I fret in my frantic city dollar mind

ages later I'm suddenly at the place in no time at all
it dawns on me it's nearly sunset
mountains hang like solid drapes all round
three giant valleys dovetail in a T-junction.
blue green carpet forests hundreds of metres below
assorted parrot calls spiral up in eucalyptus atomised air.
I walk a path of low plants scraping my shins as I brush
feet tripping on roots
one sleepy move here and no worries mate ever

then the sudden vista-to-end-all-vistas
I babble out loud and incoherent words meaning majestic
into Mount Hay I deliver myself

John Blackhawk

Previously published in an earlier form under the title 'Moving Mountains' in *Against the Currents*, Ginninderra Press, 2010

Flinders moon

Flinders Ranges hilltop, full moon eve.
Sun sinks onto horizon, bright sliver left,
its brilliant line shrinks, shrinks and disappears.
I turn around to look toward the east.

Above the purple hills, now shows a line
of yellow-orange light. It widens, grows,
ascends, now leaves the dark horizon;
a huge, deep orange ball is the full moon.

Of course, we know that full moon rise
and sunset must occur together, but
in this magic setting, darkness, stillness,
mountain top and sky, it is much more.

I am the pivot of a line from sun to moon,
my arms control their movement. I feel
connected with the cosmos and the Earth.
I trudge back to my tent – contentment filled.

David Harris

Wait Till You See Thirroul

Wait till you see the way Illawarra's escarpment
Curves around and embraces the Pacific Ocean
Sparks of delight hanging above their heads at night
As dancing stars and by day as the sweltering summer sun.

Wait till you see the spectacular formation of stratus clouds
Ascending a sunrise journey along our lush green foothills
Hovering over narrow bush tracks as if checking for injured wildlife
Before allowing a new day to birth beneath its softening mist.

Wait till you wake up and hear the sweetest birdsong
So gently ricocheting through the belly of our mountain range
That their harmonies will drift you back to sleep
Making you forget that anywhere else exists.

Wait till you see the translucent yellow glow of dawn
Electrify our metallic blue ocean horizon
Like a desert mirage shimmering its way
Towards the outstretched crescent arms of Thirroul Beach.

Wait till you see our local surfers at daybreak form a moving mandala
A joyous meditation on the simple gifts of Mother Nature
Golden sunlight on salt water; framed by Mount Bulli, Dharawal Land.
I can't wait till you see Thirroul!

Gabrielle Journey Jones

Reflections

Oozy meadows, brooding shadows, soft warm light.
Gentle windy breath scudding over bog-black lake.
High-swept clouds and immensity of sky powder-blue.
Burbling brook a constant internal conversation
With itself, of past lives and thoughts about the future.
Quiet gentle grove of whispering autumn oaks.

Out here a stark beauty, wildness quite different from,
Late summer city gardens with massive overgrowth.
Up here the air is clear and heady, distance far.
Nature is lean and brown, moulded and round
On Wicklow hills. There is a certainty in length of things.
The shortening days and coming of the winter sun.

Catharine Steinberg

Previously published in *Signs of a Poetic Life*, Ginninderra Press, 2017

Not everyone knows

In the main street of a 'subalpine' town, weekend tourists flock
for lunchtime coffee, with quiche and rocket salad. But in the quiet of back streets
red 'sold' banner adorns a yellow 'for sale' sign, that's been up for days at least.
Close to half a million, and 'bang', it's gone – who could afford that? –
while next door, and two doors up, the fence is down. Along the road a bit,
tarpaulins still grace a roof, after bloodwood branch damage, a decade old,
bent strip of stumped guttering leaks, venetians crumple
in a blank dark window. The poor are staying put.

Fallen, cut, and teetering trunks leer at empty space on the clifftop
above the river. Winter cassinia, like tall lanky rosemary bushes, without flowers,
guard a steep descent. Wombat crap on the track is a positive omen:
somewhere in their slow-thinking minds, an avoidance of motor vehicles
could be sinking in.

I love the view of eucalypt-clad hillsides, from high here, standing
on the compacted spongy loam of borer-eaten timber peat and mulched leaves,
the greyishness, the sticks of branches, the sense of relief, where there is no culture,
no streets, no homes, no cars, no electric wires. Just the rain setting in, the cold
drizzle of late winter, the roar of the river over rapids
where the 'pick, pick' of small birds dominates. Gnarls of clematis vine
crowd the track. Early wattles, leggy, extend above dark water. But where
are the kangaroos on the grass flat below? Instead, small fenced 'rented' paddocks,
requiring the felling of large mountain ash trees, sport a goat
and a sheep.

Tass Holmes

to the pyramid

It's an hour's hard-stepping ascent
we climb slowly
a tree   an orchid   a view
pretexts to catch our breath

Some pyramids you drive to and then climb
these are generally grand and imposing
places to wonder about the ancients
and confront any fear of heights

In Tepoztlán, you climb a mountain first
and the pyramid itself is small
We leave behind the Sunday strollers
boys with ghetto blasters, girls in heels

Ahead of us, those who climb often
ascend easily, they know
these cliffs and gullies
in their bones

Finally we tackle the iron ladder
emerge into the pyramid precinct
a mountain wall behind us
all our world below
a sudden hint of magic in the breeze

Jacqueline Buswell

www.ingramcontent.com/pod-product-compliance
Lightning Source LLC
Chambersburg PA
CBHW071840080526
44589CB00012B/1063